Between Damascus and Jerusalem
LEBANON AND MIDDLE EAST PEACE

Habib C. Malik

Policy Paper No. 45

THE WASHINGTON INSTITUTE FOR NEAR EAST POLICY

All rights reserved. Printed in the United States of America. No part of this publication may be reproduced or transmitted in any form or by any means, electronic or mechanical, including photocopy, recording, or any information storage and retrieval system, without permission in writing from the publisher.

© 1997 by The Washington Institute for Near East Policy

Published in 1997 in the United States of America by The Washington Institute for Near East Policy, 1828 L Street N.W. Suite 1050, Washington, DC 20036

Library of Congress Cataloging-in-Publication Data

Malik, Habib C. (Habib Charles)
    Between Damascus and Jerusalem: Lebanon and Middle East Peace/ Habib Malik
    p. cm. — (Policy papers; no. 45)
  Includes bibliographical references.
  ISBN 0-944029-70-1
    1. Lebanon—Politics and government. 2.   Lebanon—Foreign relations. I. Title.   II. Series: Policy papers (Washington Institute for Near East Policy); no. 45.
    DS87.M368 1997   97–10910
    956.9204—dc21   CIP

The Author

Habib C. Malik, a 1995 visiting fellow at The Washington Institute for Near East Policy, received his Ph.D. in modern European intellectual history from Harvard University and is currently affiliated with the Lebanese-American University (Byblos branch). He previously taught history and cultural studies at the American University of Beirut's off-campus program and philosophy at the Catholic University of America in Washington, DC.

Dr. Malik is a founding member of the Foundation for Human and Humanitarian Rights, an independent, non-governmental organization in Lebanon. He has published many articles in English and Arabic on Lebanon, the Christians of the Middle East, Christianity in the West, and human rights. His most recent book is *Receiving Søren Kierkegaard: The Early Impact and Transmission of His Thought* (Catholic University of America Press, 1997).

• • •

The opinions expressed in this Policy Paper are those of the author and should not be construed as representing those of The Washington Institute for Near East Policy, its Board of Trustees, or Board of Advisors.

Contents

Acknowledgments	ix
Preface	xi
Executive Summary	xiii
I Lebanon: History and Identities	1
II The Evaporation of Politics	25
III The Economics of Autocracy	47
IV Civil Society Fights Back	65
V Lebanon in the Context of a Syria-Israel Peace Agreement	79
VI Conclusions and Policy Recommendations	99
Appendices	111
1989 Lebanese National Reconciliation (Taif) Accord	113
1991 Treaty of Brotherhood, Cooperation, and Coordination	125
1991 Defense and Security Agreement	129

Acknowledgments

As this paper took shape I received helpful input from a variety of people and sources. I wish to express my special thanks and appreciation to the following individuals who contributed in one form or another to the completion of the project: Wail Kheir, managing director, Foundation for Human and Humanitarian Rights (Lebanon); Daniel Nassif, Washington representative of the Council of Lebanese-American Organizations; Professor Farid El Khazen, American University of Beirut; Pierre Atallah, *al-Nahar* newspaper; Imad Hajj, American Underwriters in Beirut; Pierre Abou Jaber, manager of the Bank of Kuwait & the Arab World (Beirut, Ashrafieh branch); Professor Fouad Ajami of the School of Advanced International Studies, Johns Hopkins University; Daniel Pipes, editor of *Middle East Quarterly*; and Muriel Mafrige of Washington, D.C.

I would also like to thank Rob Satloff for all his help and for the kind hospitality he extended to me during my fellowship at the Washington Institute. The senior scholars at the Institute provided invaluable suggestions as the paper evolved, and the efficient staff made my work easier every step of the way. To both these groups I offer my warmest gratitude. Lastly, all opinions and any errors in this paper are my responsibility alone.

Habib C. Malik
Beirut
July 1997

Preface

Over the past two decades, "Lebanon" became synonymous with civil war, hostage-taking, and terrorism, and a metaphor for national catastrophe and "failed states" the world over. Since the 1983 withdrawal of U.S. forces from Beirut after a radical Islamist truck-bomb killed more than 200 U.S. Marines, U.S. policymakers have generally avoided dealing with the issue of Lebanon.

Despite its relegation to the periphery of world concerns, Lebanon remains a critical setting for issues of war and peace in the Middle East. Since the 1989 Taif accord, this once-independent country has been forced to endure occupation by tens of thousands of Syrian troops as the price for ending decades of civil strife, anarchy, and war. At the same time, its border zone with Israel—where Hezbollah militants, acting on their own and as proxies for Syria and Iran, battle Israeli forces and their local allies on a daily basis—remains the last "hot" frontier in the Arab-Israeli conflict. In July 1993 and April 1996, Lebanese civilians became unwilling participants in mini-wars when Israel responded to Hezbollah rocket barrages into the Galilee with sustained air and ground reprisals.

Diplomatically, Lebanon is a participant in the Madrid peace process in name only, its decisionmakers deferring to Damascus on all issues, large and small. Tragically, America, Israel, and the Arab states seem to have reconciled themselves to Syrian control over Lebanon, allowing Damascus to achieve through ruthlessness and patience a strategic victory that would never have been attempted or tolerated through force of arms. In fact, many observers believe that retaining control over Lebanon is far more important to Syrian President Hafez al-Assad than regaining the Golan.

In this courageous and groundbreaking study, Dr. Habib C. Malik presents a comprehensive picture of political and social change during Lebanon's gradual devolution into a Syrian vassal state. He offers a sober and compelling account of the impact that *de facto* Syrian annexation has had on Lebanon's people and the region as a whole, and provides a series of realistic policy proposals that U.S. officials should consider if they are truly serious about preserving Lebanon as a sovereign, independent, and multi-communal state in the Middle East.

Although Washington and much of the world have paid little attention to Lebanon for the past two decades, it is impossible to ignore in perpetuity a country and people that have such an important role to play in the search for peace and stability in the Middle East. Hopefully, this Policy Paper will provoke considerable "new thinking" on a topic that has been overlooked for too long.

Michael Stein
President

Barbi Weinberg
Chairman

Executive Summary

It has become customary to speak of Israel-Syria peace negotiations as encompassing a Lebanese component. The interplay between Syria's hegemonic ambitions and Israel's security interests will dominate and determine Lebanon's place in whatever peace equation ultimately unfolds. In that context, there are objective justifications for Lebanon's ancillary status. But a fresh look at Lebanon itself—both internally and in relation to its two immediate neighbors—yields important insights into Middle East realities that bear directly on the outcome of the peace process.

Lebanon's unique features—including its communal heterogeneity, religious diversity (degenerating at times into sectarian strife), the asymmetry of communal fears and aspirations, and the prolonged conflict between a vibrant civil society and foreign occupation—all impact on its surroundings. Add to this the deleterious consequences of the country's collapse into anarchy and the resulting power vacuum (with their byproducts of terrorism, drug trafficking, and counterfeiting), and the picture emerges of a wide-open "playing field" in which regional rivals and conflicting international interests compete against one another.

At the core of all this is a Lebanese society comprising a patchwork of religious communities grouped under the two broad headings, Christian and Muslim. Understanding the interactive relations of these two main socio-religious groupings—and through them the shifting dynamics of Lebanon's internal fractures and fault lines—can help Washington policymakers avoid misleading stereotypes and attain a more subtle appreciation for this complex microcosm and the wider regional realities it mirrors.

The deep-seated existential phobias of Lebanon's Christians (and their corresponding absence among its Muslims) determine to a significant extent the mutual perceptions and behaviors of the two communities. As Lebanese Christians face the prospect of increased Islamicization, they react either by resisting it defiantly or assimilating more fully into the changing surroundings, even at the expense of their authenticity and basic identity. For their part, the vast majority of Lebanese Muslims prefer Beirut's free, open, and pluralist character and do not necessarily wish to exchange it for the sullen and insular environment of the more markedly Islamic cities of the region. They often lose sight, however, of the inherent connection between the Beirut they desire and the main reason it is free, open, and superior to other Islamic environments: the rooted presence in Beirut—and Lebanon as a whole—of a free, dynamic, industrious, and relatively secure native Christian community.

Following the 1989 Taif agreement and the October 1990 Syrian occupation of 90 percent of Lebanon north of Israel's self-declared security zone, the urgent task at hand became not so much figuring out how Lebanon's Christians and Muslims can live together, but rather how the basic rights and freedoms for individuals and communities regardless of their religious affiliation can be protected from the mounting ravages of the prolonged foreign (and particularly Syrian) intervention. The tightening Syrian stranglehold led to the evaporation of the freewheeling political life that was a hallmark of pre-war Lebanon. For example, Syria and its local Lebanese proxies blatantly stage-managed the parliamentary elections in 1992 and 1996.

Syria subsequently imposed a series of bilateral political, economic, and security agreements on Lebanon, with the aim of gradually absorbing the latter. Most notorious are the 1991 "Treaty of Brotherhood, Cooperation, and Coordination" and "Defense and Security Agreement," which paved the way for far-reaching Syrian meddling in nearly every aspect of Lebanon's internal affairs. A relentless process of "Syrianization" ensued that has effectively drawn new demarcation lines between Lebanon's embattled but still vibrant civil society and the forces of Syrian occupation and intimidation. Resistance to Syrianization is not confined to any one religious community in Lebanon, although clearly a Lebanon without its free and outspoken Christian community would quickly become a version of its expansionist neighbor to the east.

Post-Taif Lebanon exhibits a disturbing tapestry of artificially induced demographic imbalances, unevenly distributed reconstruction, economic mismanagement, environmental destruction, steadily eroding press freedoms, recurring government confrontations with the independent labor union, and tampering with the privately run educational sector. The increasingly porous Lebanese-Syrian border allows hundreds of thousands of Syrian workers to travel to Lebanon ostensibly seeking employment, mainly in construction. These vast numbers give Syria's military occupation and political control a quasi-colonial dimension. Add to this the 1994 Naturalization Decree, which granted Lebanese citizenship to some 300,000 mostly Syrian Muslims, and the continued presence in Lebanon of tens of thousands of Muslim Palestinians who may yet be naturalized, and Lebanon's demographic cauldron seethes ominously.

False starts and inordinate delays have marked Lebanon's post-war reconstruction, which was launched and is sustained by the country's multi-millionaire prime minister, Rafiq Hariri. Despite mounting criticisms (often from respectable economic experts), Hariri has forged ahead with massive external borrowing of hard currency to finance a reconstruction scheme that takes little account of Beirut's rich archaeological heritage or architectural cachet, attempting instead to create in the city's devastated downtown a Hong Kong-Jeddah hybrid of steel, glass, and concrete.

The Assad regime has always regarded control over Lebanon as second in importance only to its own survival, and any incentive to be forthcoming in negotiations with Israel remains severely curtailed as long as Damascus feels secure in Lebanon. Whereas Israel's security requirements *vis-à-vis* Lebanon are finite, defined by Lebanon's strategic location and role as a continuing source of terrorism, Syria's aims in Lebanon are theoretically limitless. Although Syria undoubtedly has legitimate interests in Lebanon and a stake in the country's political orientation, the depths of its intrusiveness in recent years have made a mockery of this justifiable degree of influence. Lebanon's effective status as Syria's hostage has prevented rather than facilitated a peace agreement with Israel.

For its part, Israel's policies in Lebanon underwent a three-phase evolution: from an alliance of non-Muslim minorities (ending in 1983) to a series of pragmatic "deals" with a variety of Lebanese factions (ending in 1990) to a search for a lasting bilateral arrangement with Syria. If one discounts the likelihood of the two diametric scenarios—a full and durable peace or deterioration leading to war—it becomes apparent that any kind of a partial peace or perpetuation of the status quo between Syria and Israel would readily sacrifice Lebanon's independence and sovereignty.

At a time when dictatorships and their "captive nations" are on the decline around the world, Lebanon finds itself being forced to march against the tide of history: Lebanon's satellite status with respect to Syria is one of the Middle East's most arresting anachronisms. No matter how the current situation and the near term are assessed, it is not in Washington's long-term interests for Lebanon to remain subjugated by Syria. There can be no real or lasting Middle East peace with the perpetuation of such circumstances of occupation.

Despite Lebanon's bleak current predicament, the country's eclipsed freedoms and defining characteristics can be salvaged through an incremental and multi-pronged approach. A sincere, serious, and sustained U.S. policy designed for the long term would do much to catalyze the eventual restoration of Lebanese sovereignty and communal well-being. If the intention exists, U.S. policymakers can walk a thin line that would facilitate the emergence of conditions for this restoration without impinging upon Syria's legitimate vital interests in Lebanon.

The key is to bolster Lebanon's civil society in every way possible. This would entail encouraging the gradual rise of a credible, responsible, and free opposition within the Lebanese body politic; helping to avoid a repeat of the flagrant parliamentary election farces of 1992 and 1996; continuing to call attention to human rights violations in Lebanon and making further aid contingent upon tangible improvements in the record; lending support to the autonomy of rooted institutional components of Lebanese civil society, such as the free enterprise economy, the free press, the strong educational sector, the many active and independent unions and associations; building up the Lebanese armed forces not as a tool of state repression but as an independent and patriotic institution demonstrating effective security capabilities; encouraging normalization between Lebanon and Israel once a formal peace treaty has been signed; and modifying the official American attitude to the Taif agreement to allow for substantive amendments leading toward political decentralization and a post-peace, communally grounded, federal formula for Lebanon.

I

Lebanon: History and Identities

The past twenty-two years have conditioned many people to view Lebanon in the context of (and, indeed, as a synonym for) perpetual turmoil. On several occasions during this period, events in Lebanon briefly grabbed world attention and became the focal point for larger Middle Eastern developments. The rest of the time, however, the country folded in on itself and disintegrated with a ferocity that was barely felt beyond its borders. These intermittent moments at center stage include the outbreak of the 1975-76 Palestinian-Lebanese conflict, which quickly turned into civil war and culminated in Syrian entry into the country; the 1982 Israeli invasion and the consequent introduction of multinational forces to evacuate the Palestine Liberation Organization (PLO) from Beirut; the October 1983 bombing of the U.S. Marine barracks in Beirut; the seizure and eventual release of Western hostages throughout the 1980s and early 1990s; and the Syrian army's October 1990 occupation of Lebanon's Christian areas.[1] For most of the remaining period, however, Lebanon suffered alone on the periphery of world politics.

Since the advent of the Madrid peace process following Iraq's defeat in the 1991 Gulf War, Lebanon has been the phantom participant in the negotiations. Although there have been oblique references to an eventual peace treaty between Israel and Lebanon, Syria's effective control over the Beirut government (and the diplomatic fiction that passes for official Lebanon) dictates that the actual deal be worked out in the framework of the Israel-Syria negotiating track.

Yet the "Lebanon factor" in the peace process is important in itself, and continues to play a crucial role in any prospective Israel-Syria agreement. No real and durable peace in the region can indefinitely postpone addressing the problems of Lebanon, including the kind of

---

[1] Throughout this study, the period of conflict in Lebanon from 1975 to 1990 is referred to as the "Lebanon war" rather than the more common (at least in the West) "Lebanese civil war." Strictly speaking, many features of the turmoil did not conform to the textbook definition of a civil war. It began as a Palestinian-Lebanese conflict (with the Palestinians constituting an armed foreign element on Lebanese soil) and quickly took on the sectarian trappings of civil strife, but political and military intervention by external parties—Syria, Israel, Iran, Libya, foreign mercenaries, multinational forces, and through its political and financial leverage, Saudi Arabia—was evident from the start and grew throughout. In fact, on a number of occasions, Lebanese Christians and Muslims found themselves (however fleetingly) on the *same* side of their supposed civil war, battling these external parties.

viable state it aspires to be. By the same token, Lebanon's realistic hope of eventual recovery from the ravages of prolonged internal strife and foreign occupation lies firmly embedded in the success of the peace process. The issue is therefore how Lebanon can regain its political independence, territorial sovereignty, and dwindling personal and communal freedoms that are the sources of its distinctiveness, while at the same time accommodating the security needs of both Israel and Syria and satisfying the overall requirements for regional peace.

In order to analyze current conditions inside Lebanon, assess its place in various possible scenarios for an Israel-Syria deal, and offer specific recommendations for U.S. policies that will contribute to reconstituting a free and sovereign Lebanon after peace between its powerful neighbors, some of Lebanon's defining characteristics need to be considered along with the divergent concepts of Lebanon's identity that underlie them.

"Small" and "fragile" are usually foremost among the many adjectives used to describe Lebanon and, on the whole, Lebanon has always exhibited these two traits. In describing its constituent components, however, one can add irreducibility, since Lebanon is essentially a collection of seventeen heterogeneous religious communities (divided roughly into Christian and Muslim categories)[2] that have demonstrated a remarkable resilience and durability throughout successive and often turbulent historical periods. These communities have undergone a checkered history together and have in recent times tried, with mixed success, to forge a degree of collective identity without compromising their distinctive and autonomous communal features. In the best of times, a uniquely Lebanese consociational version of democracy has emerged—something rare in the Middle East—which has conferred upon Lebanon a well-earned separateness from the rest of the region.

Lebanon is the embodiment of two fixed ideas—that ultimate identity in the Middle East (for individuals as well as groups) remains religious in essence, and that ultimate loyalties in composite societies like Lebanon are sub-national (i.e., communal). At the same time, it is handicapped by the complexity of its societal structure and the fact that it is perceived to be of marginal regional and international importance externally. Hence, Lebanon presents a four-sided matrix of religious identities, sub-national loyalties, internal complexity, and external marginality. For many Western policymakers it has been a daunting task to comprehend the interactive sum of these four factors, and few have made the effort in recent years, finding it easier instead to consign Lebanon to the fringes of Middle Eastern priorities.

Nevertheless, Lebanon continues to demand its rightful attention within the peace process. Situated as it is between Israel and Syria, the notion of quarantining it to fester in isolation no longer applies in the

---

[2] Official recognition of Lebanon's Coptic community in July 1995 raised the number to eighteen.

new, integrated regional context of (slowly) emerging peace. Examining the vicissitudes of Lebanon's diverse, communal pluralism therefore becomes unavoidable since this very same pluralism, religiously anchored on feudal-clan foundations, has been at once its unique contribution and its Achilles heel in the region.

EARLY COMMUNAL COOPERATION

Lebanon's history reveals instances of communal cooperation and conflict, as well as autonomous communal interaction with outside powers, all of which accompanied the eventual rise of the Lebanese state. In pre-technological times, Lebanon's rugged topography/terrain served as an impregnable natural refuge for a host of beleaguered and persecuted ethno-religious minorities and regional outcasts. The Lebanese mountains became the logical sanctuary for a number of communities, most notably the Druze and the Maronite Christians, both of which developed strong traditions of local autonomy. Over time these communities emerged as a collection of heterogeneous, religio-feudal family networks, the sum total of which became Lebanon as it is known today.

From the end of the sixteenth to the middle of the nineteenth centuries, a Maronite-Druze feudal association collectively controlled Mount Lebanon. The Maronite and Druze are the two Lebanese communities most historically connected to the land, and the mountain in particular. This was the period of the Imarah (Principality), which secured an impressive degree of independence in the face of centralized Ottoman rule. "During this period [1590-1842] Lebanon acquired its special character as a separate political entity with a tradition of autonomy."[3]

Following an outbreak of inter-communal massacres and the intervention of the great powers, another period of autonomy commenced in 1861 and lasted until the end of World War I. This period covered the establishment of the autonomous Sanjak of Mount Lebanon (known as the Mutasarrifiya), which witnessed a reasonably long period of peace and prosperity during which the political and administrative foundations of the future French-controlled Lebanon and the independent Republic of Lebanon were laid.[4] With the approval of the European powers overseeing the new arrangement, the Ottomans created the Administrative Council of Mount Lebanon to serve as an advisory body.

---

[3] Meir Zamir, *The Formation of Modern Lebanon* (Ithaca, NY: Cornell University Press, 1985), p. 5.
[4] The best study to date of this period is by Turkish scholar Engin Akarli, who relied on hitherto unexamined Ottoman archives relating to the Mutasarrifiya period; see Akarli, *The Long Peace: Ottoman Lebanon, 1861 to 1920* (Berkeley, CA: University of California Press, 1993). Akarli arrives at the conclusion that the Lebanese, on their own and despite socio-religious differences, were in the process of constructing the rudiments of a nation and formulating a national identity in the late nineteenth and early twentieth centuries.

The Council comprised twelve representatives elected by the *sheikhs* (village elders) and reflected a proportional representation for all the sects of the mountain: four Maronites, three Druze, two Greek Orthodox, one Greek Catholic (Melchite), and one Shi'a and one Sunni Muslim. Although the Council's powers under the designated (Christian) Ottoman governor were limited, it had great influence in the local communities and represents a successful early experiment in consensual communal powersharing. With time its elected members came not only from the leading feudal families, but also from the ranks of traders, financiers, and entrepreneurs. In order to preserve economic privileges and maximize personal and communal benefits, "a process of bargains and alliances at the top"[5]—the convoluted art of political compromise that became a hallmark of Lebanese politics in better interludes—was developed and fine-tuned during this period.

The collapse of Ottoman rule in the Arab Middle East at the end of World War I led to a division of the region by the victorious European powers into zones of influence, with the territory of Lebanon and Syria being apportioned to the French. The Christians, and especially the Maronites, had been steadily growing in numbers and expanding south from their central and northern mountain home base since the mid-nineteenth century and throughout the Mutasarrifiya period, while attaining greater economic power and overall self-confidence. The Maronite church and its patriarchate became firmly rooted institutions counterbalancing the traditional feudal families and run increasingly by an educated clergy. The community's ties to Catholic Europe were strong and, coupled with Maronite articulation of a national identity, emboldened church leaders to press for the creation of a larger Lebanese entity that could embody their national aspirations.[6] In 1920, after much lobbying in Beirut, Paris, and the Vatican by the Maronite Christians, the French created "Greater Lebanon" by adding the areas to the north, south, and east (i.e., the Bekaa Valley) to the mountain core.

The Maronites who favored Greater Lebanon were convinced that, although it diluted the relative homogeneity of the mountain, its disparate communities would retain a distinctive Christian flavor bolstered by European influence. Their demand for a larger, more viable state can be understood only in the context of the suffering they endured during World War I, particularly a famine that demonstrated the need to add agricultural territory to the mountains to enhance self-sufficiency. Potentially destabilizing demographic and ideological trends were overlooked, however, or at least fatefully submerged beneath layers of determined optimism. "Their conviction was so powerful that they totally

---

[5] Albert Hourani, "Ideologies of the Mountain and the City: Reflections on the Lebanese Civil War," in *The Emergence of the Modern Middle East* (Berkeley, CA: University of California Press, 1981), p. 172.

[6] Hourani, "Lebanon: The Development of a Political Society," in ibid., pp. 132-33.

ignored the implications of such a demand; namely, the inclusion of a large Muslim population within the larger entity."[7]

Yet notwithstanding all its pitfalls, Greater Lebanon fared reasonably well in the hostile environment of the Middle East—that is, as long as France was there to oversee it. The French Mandate produced the 1926 constitution, which granted Lebanon a parliamentary system that accommodated its communal pluralism through proportional confessional representation—again, something unique throughout the region. The subsequent organization of the state bureaucracy included the unlegislated practice established in the 1930s (and still operative today) of dividing key government posts along communal lines—a Maronite president, Sunni prime minister, and a Shi'a speaker of parliament.

But the period of French rule between 1920 and the mid-1940s also saw the emergence of two diverging trends: a consolidation of confessional politics through interconfessional deals in the Mutasarrifiya tradition, culminating in open Maronite-Sunni coordination to end French rule; and the simultaneous appearance of new nationalist and pan-Arab ideological demarcation lines running along sectarian boundaries and revealing ominous incompatibilities among communal political agendas.

This polarity between a penchant for dealmaking and compromise on one hand and a sense of distinctiveness on the other is the hallmark of Lebanese politics. The emergence of the independent Republic of Lebanon in 1943 represents a classic instance of this dialectic in operation. Although Lebanon's independence came about principally because the British ousted the French from the Levant during World War II as part of their campaign to weaken the Vichy government, tactical alliances among communities also played a role. The idea of an independent Lebanon (in addition to considerable anti-French sentiment) temporarily subsumed the otherwise disparate aspirations of the Christian and Muslim communities: the Muslims were willing to temporarily suspend their pan-Arab aspirations as a means to end direct European control; the Christians were (overly) confident in their ability to strike a deal with the Muslims after the French were gone and fulfill their dreams of an independent Christian-oriented nation. The result was the unwritten National Pact of 1943 between the leading Sunni Muslim and the Maronite Christian communities. Although its subtext maintained the divergent definitions of communal identity and religious allegiances, the agreement provided the framework for creating an independent Lebanon next to other emerging Arab states in the post-war Middle East.

After Lebanon's independence, however, successive waves of external agitation destabilized its delicate political fabric and stirred the latent embers of sectarian discord. In the 1950s and 1960s, for example, Gamal Abdel Nasser's pan-Arabist ideology appealed to Lebanese Sunnis and put the Pact's viability to a severe test; only direct U.S. military intervention in

---

[7] Zamir, *Formation of Modern Lebanon*, p. 37.

1958 resolved the crisis. Indeed, "in times of crisis, the Pact regains pre-1943 communal interpretations which mirror sectarian discord rather than unity."[8] In the late 1960s and 1970s, the PLO shifted its base of operations to Beirut after being ousted from Jordan in 1970, and relied on a combination of Palestinian refugee disaffection and local Muslim sympathy and support. In the 1980s and 1990s, militant Islamic fundamentalism inspired by the Iranian revolution came to the fore, stirring the Lebanese Shi'a and generally radicalizing Islamic political discourse across the board.

Meanwhile, Lebanon's domestic socio-economic and demographic disparities—particularly among its Muslim communities—were steadily growing and adding to the internal polarization. Thus, when the Lebanon war broke out in 1975, the National Pact quickly crumbled and initiated a process of disintegration that continued until November 1989, when a U.S.-brokered and Saudi-sponsored agreement inaugurated in Taif, Saudi Arabia, ushered in a new and precarious era of apparent stability enforced increasingly at the expense of basic freedoms and rights.

This brief historical survey demonstrates a number of constants about Lebanon. The first is that the heterogeneous religious communities are the permanent components of any Lebanese state or political superstructure, and their ability to form coalitions based on compromises or the temporary suspension of particular agendas ultimately decides the health and fate of the Lebanese state.

Second, such pragmatic dealmaking among the communities, though potentially workable, remains delicate and prone to periodic shake-ups due to the influence of regional and international forces. Moreover, it is invariably external powers—usually the West—that create the new conditions for putting the Lebanese "Humpty Dumpty" back together again each time. In recent history, direct intervention by the big powers in the wake of a shattering crisis has been the decisive factor in reconstituting the Lebanese polity.[9]

Third, beyond a collective Lebanese sociological identity that manifests itself to outsiders (including other Arabs) and involves shared similarities in mannerisms, temperament, dialect, dress, and a host of corresponding civic and economic unifiers transcending religious divides, there exists

---

[8] Farid El-Khazen, *The Communal Pact of National Identities: The Making and Politics of the 1943 National Pact*, Papers on Lebanon no. 12 (Oxford, UK: Centre for Lebanese Studies, 1991), p. 67.

[9] In 1861, a group of European powers and the Ottoman Empire brought about the Mutasarrifiya; in 1920, following the Sykes-Picot agreement, France created "Greater Lebanon." In 1943, Britain expelled the Vichy French and the independent Republic of Lebanon was born. In 1958, the U.S. Marines averted an all-out civil war and brought order to Lebanon. And between 1975 and 1989, a series of half-hearted international initiatives attempted to contain the war in Lebanon, culminating in the Taif agreement. Of all the settlements going back to 1861, only Taif broke the previous pattern of internationalizing the solutions to Lebanese crises, in favor of a regional "Arab" solution involving first Saudi Arabia and eventually Syria.

precious little to act as a substantive assimilator of Lebanon's various communities. As in every divided or composite society, each religious community develops over time its own (mis)perceptions of the others and of its place in the larger unifying entity. Sub-national differences operate decisively to generate incongruous communal self-portraits and depictions of the other; general perceptions in turn spawn particular fears and phobias that become articulated in specific and deeply ingrained threat perceptions, which then serve as the bases for a variety of communal political strategies that are at best divergent, if not clashing.

After a brief hiatus this century during which disparate secular ideologies and nationalisms emerged as the competing claimants to people's ultimate loyalties in the region, the Middle East has returned full circle to religion as the principal criterion of basic identity. Although this revived emphasis on religion has not resulted in the subversion of the nation-state system, it does point to secularism's inherent limits within a Middle Eastern context, and Lebanon is no exception in this regard.

THE CHRISTIANS

By dint of its composition, Lebanon has long lent itself to uniquely devised formulas of cultural and political expression. The separateness and distinctiveness it displays in the region comes from a combination of unique geography, sociological structure, and polity—in short, an intrinsic communal pluralism. At the root of this distinctiveness, however, is the fact that Lebanon is the only remaining place in the entire Middle East—and indeed in the whole of Asia—that is home to a free, indigenous, and sizable Christian community. The Lebanese Christian community has been rooted in the land since the early centuries of Christianity and has managed, due mainly to the stubborn dynamism of its principal sub-group, the Maronites, and at considerable cost, to preserve a carefully cultivated tradition of freedom that Albert Hourani called "rural liberty."[10] This phenomenon has left its imprint on the non-Christian communities of Lebanon that have had prolonged contact with it, rendering them markedly different in a variety of ways from their co-religionists throughout the region. Indeed, pre-1975 Lebanon enjoyed a lively, liberal, and pluralist society the likes of which the Middle East has never seen before or since.

For the Lebanese Christians (particularly but not exclusively the Maronites), Lebanon as an independent national homeland where they have lived freely has become akin to an atavism. In the face of recurrent persecution directed at Middle Eastern Christians throughout the centuries, Lebanon as a bastion of freedom became for its Christian

---

[10] Hourani, "Lebanon: The Development of a Political Society" in *Emergence of Modern Middle East*, p. 124.

inhabitants something approaching an act of faith. To these Christians, therefore, the story of Lebanon's recent turmoil remains incomprehensible unless viewed as "the drama of freedom under siege."[11]

Existentialist rhetoric aside, this illustrates an example—unique to the region—of open defiance by a native, non-Muslim minority of the Islamic category known as the *dhimmi*. Classical *shari'a* (Islamic law and jurisprudence) relegates the so-called "people of the book" (Jews and Christians) living in the "Abode of Islam" (*Dar al-Islam*)—anywhere Muslims exist in overwhelming numbers and exercise political control—to an inferior second-class status.[12] Over the centuries, Islamic conquests of one form or another have systematically reduced the Christian populations of the Middle East, with the exception of those living on Mount Lebanon, to *dhimmis* in their own lands.[13]

Although Islam's reputed tolerance allows *dhimmis* a certain degree of personal and communal self-fulfillment within their own group, they can never attain equality with the Muslims, especially in the political, legal, and financial realms. In return for "protection" that could be suspended under various conditions (depending often merely on the caprice of individual rulers), the *dhimmis* were expected to acknowledge the supremacy of Muslims and to demonstrate their submission by paying certain taxes, not bearing arms, and accepting other disabling restrictions.[14] Even in Islamic countries where *shari'a* is not implemented and legislation of *dhimmi* status has been abolished or superseded by modern constitutions and laws, the debilitating psychological vestiges of centuries of inferiorization continue to characterize non-Muslim communities. Moreover, sporadic persecutions continue. Egyptian Copts and the Christians of southern Sudan are living and tragic examples of this.

None of the elements of the *dhimmi* specter were allowed to hold permanent sway over Lebanon's Christians, even under the most difficult

---

[11] For a review essay on Arab Christians, see Habib Malik's critique of Kenneth Cragg's *The Arab Christian: A History in the Middle East* in *Beirut Review* 3 (Spring 1992) pp. 109-22. See also Malik, "The Future of Christian Arabs," in *Mediterranean Quarterly: A Journal of Global Issues* 2, no. 2 (Spring 1991), pp. 72-84.

[12] For a concise discussion of the "two abodes" concept in Islam, see Bernard Lewis, *The Muslim Discovery of Europe* (New York: W. W. Norton & Company, 1982), particularly the section entitled "The Muslim View of the World," pp. 59-69.

[13] As Bat Ye'or aptly describes it, they have undergone a gradual process of decimation mixed with fossilization; see Bat Ye'or, *The Dhimmi: Jews and Christians Under Islam*, (in French) trans. David Maisel (London: Fairleigh Dickinson University Press, 1985), p. 133.

[14] On *dhimmi* disabilities, see Bernard Lewis, *Islam and the West* (New York: Oxford University Press, 1993), pp. 47-48. For some modern Muslim perspectives on the issue, see P. J. Vatikiotis, "Non-Muslims in Muslim Society: A Preliminary Consideration of the Problem on the Basis of Recent Published Works by Muslim Authors," in eds. Milton J. Esman and Itamar Rabinovich, *Ethnicity, Pluralism, and the State in the Middle East* (Ithaca, NY: Cornell University Press, 1988), pp. 54-70. See also Yaqub Ibn Rahma, "Clients or Citizens: Non-Muslims Under Islamic Rule," an unpublished paper presented to the International Institute for the Study of Islam and Christianity in London in 1990, p. 1.

periods of Islamic rule. Indeed, Mount Lebanon's rugged summits and narrow valleys managed to preserve a considerable amount of autonomy where "a kind of free zone for spiritual products" was maintained.[15] Precisely because of their long history of resisting *dhimmi* status, the Lebanese Christians developed a special set of apprehensions that shaped their perceptions of themselves and their wider environment, including the Muslim communities with whom they shared Lebanon. On some issues there were clear inter-Christian variations of outlook, but all were beset by an inherited feeling of existential insecurity that required constant amelioration.

The Maronite church and its monastic orders down through the centuries played a central role in defending Christian freedoms and heightening Christian awareness of them. The Maronite church's role as the national church of Lebanon is similar to that of the Lutheran church in many northern European countries, the Orthodox church in Russia, and the Catholic Church in Poland and Ireland—or, for that matter, the role Shi'ism plays in Iran or Sunni Islam in Turkey[16]—it confers an indelible mark, a distinctive flavor on the place. Recognition of this special Maronite role—and even primacy—spread to members of other Christian denominations in Lebanon, but there remains a greater sense of communal cohesion and a more developed notion of collective destiny among the Maronites than among Lebanon's Greek Orthodox, Uniate Catholics, or any other Christian denomination.

This difference is reflected in the contrasting attitudes—resistance or resignation—that various Lebanese Christians assume in response to the common threat they perceive, namely Islamicization. Those advocating resistance are not averse to studied compromises and accommodations with the Muslims, as long as they can secure solid guarantees to protect the freedoms, distinctive features, and dignity of their community. Many of the architects of the Maronite-Sunni National Pact of 1943, for example, belonged to this category, as do some of the founders of particular Christian-dominated political parties.

Pure "resignationists" or assimilationists, on the other hand, usually believe in open-ended accommodation with a very elastic notion of the concessions they are prepared to offer. Examples include various strands of ideological Arabists and those who promote the idea of a "Greater Syria." Most of the Maronites (as well as unspecified segments of other Christian denominations) have followed the former and predominant trend; some Orthodox or Protestant intellectuals and their followers, certain wealthy urban-dwellers anxious to preserve lucrative business connections, and an assortment of individuals and isolated subgroups

---

[15] The expression comes from Wail Kheir, "The Downfall of Lebanese Christianity: What Does it Mean?," an unpublished tract submitted to the Middle East Council of Churches in 1985.
[16] Ibid.

comprise the latter, which comes closer to a form of quasi-*dhimmi* status. Interestingly, the position of one Christian group is very often motivated more by a desire to set itself apart from another Christian tendency than to resist or accommodate the Muslims.

Traditional Christian resistance to Islamicization and various interim stages of "*dhimmi*tude" has taken many forms that were overwhelmingly socio-cultural in nature, and only rarely as the last resort assumed a military character. Maronite monasticism, with its combined emphasis on ascetic isolation from the world and involvement in it through education, represented a pivotal form of this resistance. The subsequent flourishing of Catholic and Protestant missionary schools and institutions, which transformed Lebanon into a regional educational hub, reinforced Christian ascendancy in the field of learning while simultaneously creating opportunities for greater numbers of Muslims in and around Lebanon to receive a liberal education, thereby exposing them to new horizons beyond the strict confines of their native faith.

Likewise, the historical links to Europe the Maronites cultivated were intended among other things to preserve a "lifeline" to Christian civilization in the West as a hedge against the threat of regional assimilation or absorption.[17] Another strategy against absorption was to maintain use of Syriac as the liturgical language, while at the same time embracing Arabic in such a way that by the end of the nineteenth century Maronite and other Christian scholars and intellectuals from Lebanon were responsible for major contributions in that language, as well as translations to and from it. Furthermore, the steady Maronite commercial and demographic expansion into the urban centers along Lebanon's coast that had been ongoing since the latter part of the nineteenth century, did not preclude the continued nurturing of a mountain village culture with traditions of family cohesiveness and close clan-church relations. These served as reservoirs of authentic identity and attachment to the ancestral land that offset the perils of displacement and uprootedness. But at times they also enhanced an insular form of localism that approached the parochial.

By contrast, the assimilationist Christians have been driven to resignation by a curious blend of fear, sycophancy, and mercantilism. Their attitudes toward the Muslims are perhaps best summed up by the motto: "Don't rock the boat at any cost." They have internalized the *dhimmi* mentality to such an extent that it has replaced whatever truncated identity they may have had to start with. This tragedy reached its climax when they awakened to find that, despite their efforts at appeasement, resurgent Islamists regard them no differently from other Christians. A few decided to convert to Islam; most simply dropped out of public life. The

---

[17] An important reason for strengthening their Western contacts was that, unlike most other eastern Christians, the Maronites have been in doctrinal communion with the Roman Catholic church since the year 1180.

few who remained politically active became unabashed mouthpieces for Arab influence (Saudi Arabia) or occupation (Syria), and lack any popular base of support among their fellow Christians.

The Christians of Lebanon entered active political life in the early twentieth century, and particularly after 1943, in a manner unprecedented for their co-religionists in the region since the days of Byzantium. Contrary to prevailing misconceptions and popular stereotypes generated by Western journalists with undisguised anti-Christian biases,[18] the Lebanese Christians—including the Maronites—for the most part did not view their political ascendancy in triumphalist terms or as a means to protect their supposed "privileges" and perpetuate a hegemonic posture. Rather, they felt they needed guarantees and other protections to prevent a gradual slide down the perilous *dhimmi* slope, and in addition to employing numerous strategies of resistance, secured these through the posts of president of the republic, commander of the army, and the foreign affairs portfolio in the government. Lebanon's pre-Taif constitution gave the president a wide range of executive powers that were rarely invoked in full, but whose mere presence in the law reassured the Christians and helped to assuage somewhat their latent fears. Given Lebanon's post-independence history, many Christians would concur that these existential fears, gnawing relentlessly on both their individual and collective psyches, were entirely justified.

This is not to overlook the frequent and glaring failures of Lebanese Christian political and spiritual leadership in times of crisis. Before and during the Lebanon war, the roster of missed opportunities, bungled attempts, incessant infighting, and corrupt practices in which Christian leaders indulged has been sadly long. Responding to unwarranted and factually erroneous attacks on the Christian community as a whole and calling attention to the underlying fears and existential issues at stake in the fateful historical drama it has endured does not excuse the shortsightedness and ineptitude of particular figures or political parties at various points in time. Neither lamentations nor condemnations address the essence of the Lebanese Christian predicament—a set of very real anxieties about freedom and dignity that surface periodically and often lead to devastating consequences when mishandled—which can be said to constitute the core of the Lebanon problem.

The Sunni Muslims insisted in 1943 that the Christians accept the formulation "Lebanon with an Arab face" as a precondition for entering into the National Pact. This formulation seemed a reasonable compromise

---

[18] One notorious example of this genre of writing bordering on racism is Jonathan C. Randal's *Going All the Way: Christian Warlords, Israeli Adventurers, and the War in Lebanon* (New York: Viking Press, 1983). Another, more recent specimen of journalism about Lebanon's Christians still does not capture the crucial nuances that would bring out the complexity of their plight (and that of Lebanon as well); see "Dreaming of Christian Lebanon," *Economist*, June 17, 1995. There is certainly room for a scholarly study deconstructing distorted depictions of Lebanon's Christians.

at the time because it implied that Lebanon had other faces as well. Nasser's pan-Arabist rallying cry in the 1950s and 1960s resonated emotionally with Lebanon's Sunnis, and they began to clamor for the more direct, and therefore more menacing, assertion that Lebanon is Arab. The ominous implication that "Arab" could be a synonym for "Muslim" precipitated Christian resistance and led in 1958 to the first major post-independence sectarian crisis.

The theme of "Arab Lebanon" continued in the context of galvanized Lebanese Muslim support for the PLO.[19] The outbreak of the Lebanon war in 1975, coupled with sectarian killings, the wholesale displacement of populations, and destruction of villages by both sides—Lebanon's version of "ethnic cleansing"—led to outright calls for an Islamic Lebanon from certain Muslim leaders.[20] The 1979 Islamic revolution in Iran and its powerful regional repercussions ignited the Lebanese Shi'a community, which had already been radicalized by years of poverty and neglect. Iran—followed by Hezbollah, Hamas, Sudan, Algeria, and Islamist threats to Egypt—ushered in an era of Islamic fundamentalism in which previous innuendoes were abandoned in favor of unequivocal demands by a militants seeking Islamic rule in Lebanon and elsewhere. Naturally, there were moderate Muslims who recoiled at this prospect, but the record of Islamic moderation is at best uneven and at worst pathetically impotent in the face of the vocal and determined militancy of a few well-organized fanatics supported and financed from outside.

Seen through Lebanese Christian eyes, two events transformed this post-independence "slippery slope" of deterioration into a full-fledged defeat: the Taif agreement, and the devastating 1990 inter-Christian fighting that paved the way for Syrian occupation of Lebanon north of Israel's self-declared security zone.[21] With a growing feeling of unease,

---

[19] See the Arabic text of the proceedings of meetings and the statements of a coalition of Lebanese Muslim political and religious leaders including the late Sunni Mufti Hassan Khaled, the charismatic Shi'a cleric Musa al-Sadr, and Yasser Arafat in *Al-Muslimun fi Lubnan wal Harb al-Ahliyya: Mahadir Ijtima'at Qimmat 'Aramun* (The Muslims in Lebanon and the Civil War: Minutes of the 'Aramun Summit Meetings), by the Mufti Sheikh Hassan Khaled of *Dar al-Ifta* (Beirut: Kindi Publishing House, 1978), especially pp. 92-96, 244-50.

[20] See, for example, the notorious article by the director general of the Sunni Mufti's office, Hussein Quwatli, published in *al-Safir*, August 18, 1975. Quwatli, an authoritative voice, says openly and accurately that exercising political control is an integral part of Islam, just as it is to wage holy war against infidels and reduce Christians and Jews to *dhimmis*. Needless to say, the article caused ripples of panic among the embattled Christians.

[21] Contrary to a prevailing and erroneous impression that the Christians were hopelessly divided in 1990 and ended up viciously slaughtering one another, the overwhelming majority of Christians (along with many Muslims) rallied around General Michel Aoun, whose movement was subverted by a determined handful of militia leaders led by Samir Geagea and backed by a few heavily armed followers who lacked any significant popular support. One beneficial by-product of the Aoun populist movement was that it effectively rid Lebanon (and the Christian community in particular) of an insidious form of homespun fascism emerging and spreading in their midst, and represented by the remnants of the Christian militia known as the Lebanese Forces.

weary Christians continue to view themselves as the targets of malevolent forces of Islamicization and Syrianization.[22] The undeniable degree of intercommunal estrangement, exacerbated by years of separation and conflict and approaching in some instances stark alienation, has rendered all attempts at genuine national reconciliation between Christians and Muslims, particularly in the shadow of Taif and Syrian occupation, sour and elusive. A combination of *ennui*, demoralization, a sense of abandonment, and intimidation has befallen the Christians. Their political and religious leaders have shown themselves time and again to be less than adequate, contentiously petty, and generally out of touch with the subtleties of regional and international politics. Attrition through emigration has taken a heavy toll, including the loss of much of the qualitative advantage that had distinguished the community in the past. Many of those who remain joylessly pursue a pragmatic coexistence with their Muslim counterparts predicated on the minimalist motive of mutual economic benefit.

THE MUSLIMS

If the fears and insecurities of Lebanese Christians are existential, those preoccupying Lebanon's Muslims do not exceed the level of communal grievances and complaints—albeit often very legitimate ones. This qualitative asymmetry in the anxieties and threat perceptions between the two essential components of the Lebanese polity is a crucial element in the Lebanese dilemma. Whereas the Christians' ultimate worries have to do with freedom, maintaining a distinctive socio-cultural identity, resisting the subjugation to an inferior status (that is, worries of the "to be or not to be" kind), Muslim concerns do not surpass the social, economic, and political spheres, and hardly ever reach dimensions of destiny and survival. The reasons for this imbalance are simple and straightforward: the overwhelming regional numerical superiority of the Muslims, combined with a preponderance of territory and resources; the history of Islamic conquests and occasional persecutions of non-Muslims; the fragile record of freedom—however imperfect—that Lebanese Christians have labored to preserve; and the unreliability of external support for bolstering such freedom.[23]

---

[22] Some examples of perceived targeting include the continued exile of Gen. Aoun and other Christian leaders in Paris, a February 1994 explosion in a church which killed and injured a number of worshipers, the trial and imprisonment of militia chief Samir Geagea and the disbanding of his paramilitary organization, a failed attempt in 1994 to split Dory Chamoun's National Liberal Party by wooing his niece, the weakening of the Phalange (Kataeb) Party, and repeated pressures on the Maronite Patriarch to soften his criticisms.

[23] To speak of "Muslims" or "Islam" in monolithic terms is obviously misleading. There are many variations of Islam and a correspondingly diverse community of Muslims, and these distinctions must be factored into any serious analysis of the faith and its adherents. There

The absence of existential fears among Lebanon's Muslims, and the uniformity of outlook they tend to display with respect to the Christians, are most starkly in evidence in times of crisis. In 1920, for example, the Sunni Muslim inhabitants of the coastal cities of Tripoli, Beirut, and Sidon expressed vehement opposition to the creation of "Greater Lebanon," favoring instead union with Syria. This opposition recurred in different forms throughout the 1920s and 1930s, abating only when common opposition to the French Mandate permitted a Sunni-Maronite rapprochement during the 1940s.[24] The Sunnis had always objected to the special status of Mount Lebanon under the Mutasarrifiya, and the fact that the Ottoman Turks were themselves Sunnis did not assuage the psychological frustration of the indigenous Sunni population of the Lebanese coast or the Syrian interior caused by the end of their centuries-long rule over the region. In the aftermath of the Ottoman demise, therefore, the Franco-Maronite "Greater Lebanon" seemed to the Sunnis (and other Muslim communities, inasmuch as they were able to articulate their feelings) the final affront.

The Muslims suspected Lebanon's Christians (and particularly the Maronites) of preferring close association with foreign "Christian" powers to Arab connections. During times of tension or confrontation, they depicted Christians in cruder terms as neo-Crusaders, fifth columnists, and agents of imperialism. The Christians themselves often unwittingly seemed to confirm some of these accusations—for example in the overtly pro-Western policies of certain Christian-dominated Lebanese governments, the excessive zeal of some Christians in embracing Western culture while simultaneously denigrating things Arab, incriminating alliances (such as with Israel prior to and during its 1982 invasion of Lebanon) forged usually when the community is under severe strain, and the sporadic popularity in Christian circles of ideologies such as Phoenicianism, Mediterraneanism, or some version of Lebanese nationalism designed to counteract or dilute the rise and popularity of opposing ideologies like Arab nationalism, pan-Arabism, and Greater Syria.

Another Christian tendency that emerges in times of upheaval and triggers serious Muslim concerns is an insular bid for self-sufficiency within a "fortress" Christian enclave. This Muslims view this as a dangerous form of separatism and exclusivism—an attempt by the Christians to "go it alone" and create their own state. The Muslims and their Palestinian and Leftist allies derisively referred to the Christians during the Lebanon war

---

is a remarkable degree of uniformity, however, in Islamic views of "the other"—that is, non-Muslims. The inalterable nature of the Koran and early traditions (e.g., the dualism of the "Two Abodes" concept), the jurisprudential infrastructure, historical practice, popular mindset, and the *dhimmi* classification effectively offset the otherwise varied manifestations of Islam that Muslims themselves represent, and thus in the context of their relationship to non-Muslims, it is not as much of an oversimplification to refer to an "Islamic view" or "Muslim outlook."

[24] See El-Khazen, *Communal Pact of National Identities*, pp. 10-16.

as "isolationists." Hence the greatest sin in the eyes of Lebanese Muslims is partition: the deliberate division of the country into mini-states and the carving out of religious cantons.

Since Taif, it has become a standard refrain in Muslim circles (and among the Shi'a specifically) to call for replacing Lebanon's system of political sectarianism with one that favors numerical majorities. The Muslims feel this system of political sectarianism has acted only to preserve and perpetuate Christian privileges and political preeminence. Muslim confidence in numerical superiority over the long term, and the notion among some that the war in Lebanon did finally produce victors and vanquished (with their side among the former), have caused many Muslims to reject political sectarianism in favor of deconfessionalization.

The Christians' tactical reply has been two-pronged. First, they point out that the call for ending the political sectarian system of apportioning government and civil service posts emanates largely from a single religious group—the Muslims—and as such is itself unacceptably sectarian. Second, rather than a half-measure that simply substitutes religious demographics for religious affiliation, the Christians say, Lebanon should adopt a thoroughly secular system that completely separates religion from politics. This proposal effectively terminates the entire debate, however, because secularism risks tampering with Islamic legal definitions of personal status. (The Muslims already feel they have made a major concession by agreeing to the absence of any reference to a "state religion" in the Lebanese constitution—all other Arab constitutions refer to Islam as the official religion of the state.) As a result, things remain exactly as they are.[25]

These recurring disagreements over issues of national import reveal an underlying and persistent tendency among the Muslims: the need to attain and maintain political domination. Although there are no specific guidelines regarding how to do so, this need to have and retain political control appears intrinsic to Islam. It is therefore much easier for Muslims to grant the non-Muslims a degree of autonomy in personal and communal affairs—even the *dhimmi* system provides for some of this—than to allow them to achieve complete political self-fulfillment.

The two main Muslim communities in Lebanon, the Sunni and the Shi'a, have each demonstrated in peculiar ways the desire to augment their political power and socio-economic standing. After a journey through the ideological landscapes of Nasserism, Arabism, and Palestinianism, and following years of internal conflict that shook the very foundations of its cozy arrangement with the Maronites since 1943, the Sunni community has emerged more self-confident about its own future and quite happy with

---

[25] The series of arguments and counterarguments about deconfessionalization and secularism leading to deadlock and a perpetuation of the status quo is described in Kamal Salibi, *A House of Many Mansions: The History of Lebanon Reconsidered* (Berkeley, CA: University of California Press, 1988), pp. 196-97. For a discussion of the roots of Lebanon's confessional system, see John P. Entelis, *Pluralism and Party Transformation in Lebanon: Al-Kataib 1936-1970* (Leiden, Netherlands: E. J. Brill, 1974), pp. 1-8, 17-27.

the status quo. For the Sunnis, the Taif agreement represented the first step toward the rehabilitation of their political status as a community. Expectations were greatly heightened in the fall of 1992 when Rafiq Hariri, a wealthy Sunni businessman from Sidon with strong Saudi connections, became prime minister.

Long before he assumed the top Sunni post in government, Hariri had been courting the Sunni community in the social and economic domains. Hariri-funded scholarships for Sunni students, and a number of economic and institutional projects undertaken by the private Hariri Foundation to improve the overall welfare of the community, ensured him broad-based support and paved the way for his grand entry into Lebanese politics. Although Hariri's swift rise to prominence overshadowed the traditional Sunni political personalities, the wealthy and established Sunni families by and large began to feel the steady ascendancy of their community and suddenly, as if born again, they discovered Lebanon and pride in being Lebanese. This new-found Sunni-style patriotism, which is not a monopoly only of the rich, includes the following ingredients: unconditional support for a unified Lebanon, acceptance of the more subordinate role for the Christians brought about by Taif, rejection in theory of political sectarianism (even though the Sunni political establishment continues to practice it), and wariness of radical Islamic militancy of any kind.

By contrast, the Shi'a community has been less wary of religious militancy. Since the early 1970s and during the long years of the Lebanon war, the Shi'a experienced a full-fledged coming of age. Many factors helped to crystallize this heightened self-consciousness. The Shi'a shift from relative obscurity to restless assertiveness occurred mainly as a result of charismatic cleric Imam Musa al-Sadr. The tall and imposing Iran-born Shi'a *mullah* moved to Lebanon in 1959 and quickly developed a following among lower class Shi'a who saw themselves as downtrodden and deprived. The Amal ("Hope") movement, which began as a paramilitary organization during the war as the Shi'a answer to the other armed sectarian militias (before the arrival of Hezbollah) was later transformed into a political party embodying Musa al-Sadr's legacy. Its leader, Nabih Berri, had been one of al-Sadr's protégés and eventually became speaker of the Lebanese parliament after the war.

In August 1978, al-Sadr disappeared mysteriously while on a trip to Libya, but not before having ignited the Lebanese Shi'a community into a fiery rage of expectation. Fouad Ajami captured the tragic poignancy of the situation: "Sayyid Musa helped stir up a storm, and when the storm came, he was one of its victims."[26] Thereafter, events quickly radicalized Lebanon's Shi'a. The following year Ayatollah Khomeini toppled the Shah of Iran and set up an Islamic republic in his place, providing a powerful spiritual inspiration. Israel's continued bombardment of Shi'a villages in

---

[26] Fouad Ajami, *The Vanished Imam: Musa al-Sadr and the Shia of Lebanon* (Ithaca, NY: Cornell University Press, 1986), p. 219.

southern Lebanon in retaliation for attacks against it by Palestinian fighters entrenched in the region further angered the Shi'a population and offered a political focus for their Khomeini-inspired fervor.

Following Israel's 1982 invasion of Lebanon, Shi'a political activism took on a military component with the birth of the Hezbollah (Party of God) militia. Shi'a political rhetoric now became unabashedly Islamic and anti-Western, directed mainly against the United States and Israel.[27] Since the 1960s, Khomeini had regarded all problems of Islam as stemming from the United States and Israel, and to him Lebanon and especially Beirut were the "battle ground *par excellence* where Islam confronted Western encroachment in the Middle East, with the United States and Israel constituting the spearhead of this encroachment."[28] Under this rubric, Beirut was the "corrupter of Islam since it was the major center through which Western-American culture was disseminated in the Middle East."[29]

Hezbollah leaders have at times deemed it expedient to be candid and forthcoming about their real opinion of Lebanon, preaching an Islamic state as its ultimate objective and expressing undisguised disdain for the extant order as a merely transitory stage along the way to fulfilling that aim. At other times, however, they have considered it more expedient to deny any such intention. Therefore, any denial by Hezbollah leaders of their contemptuous and antagonistic view of Lebanon is best seen in the context of a deliberately cultivated attitude of "precautionary dissimulation" (*taqiyya*) that is characteristic of Shi'a Islam.[30]

Hezbollah's appeal in the Shi'a community has rested not only on the open confrontation with Israel, but more concretely on an assortment of social, educational, and medical services designed to address the Shi'a self-image of being underprivileged and violated by an unfair Lebanese system that has purposely kept them deprived. The deeply harbored Shi'a sense of grievance against what they regard as a Sunni-Maronite condominium in Lebanon has been nurtured and exploited to the fullest extent in subtle ways by Hezbollah and its financial backers in Tehran. "In the fundamentalist scheme," writes V. S. Naipaul, "the world constantly decays and has constantly to be re-created."[31]

---

[27] For a thorough exposé of Hezbollah's worldview and attitudes toward the West, see Martin Kramer, *Hezbollah's Vision of the West*, Policy Paper no. 16 (Washington, DC: Washington Institute for Near East Policy, 1989). See also Waddah Sharara, *Dawlat Hizbullah: Lubnan Muj'tama'n Islamiyya'n* (Beirut: al-Nahar Publishing, 1996).

[28] Christos P. Ioannides, *America's Iran Injury and Catharsis* (New York: University of America Press, 1984), p. 132. In an interview on Lebanese television (September 24, 1995), Hezbollah leader Sayyid Hassan Nasrallah openly announced its goal of creating an Islamic republic in Lebanon. On its contempt for Lebanon, see Kramer, *Hezbollah's Vision of the West*, pp. 19, 25-35.

[29] Ibid.

[30] David Pryce-Jones, *The Closed Circle: An Interpretation of the Arabs* (New York: Harper and Row, 1989), p. 41.

[31] V. S. Naipaul, *Among the Believers: An Islamic Journey* (London: Penguin Books, 1982), p. 157.

Hezbollah and Islamic fundamentalism notwithstanding, the vast majority of Lebanon's Muslims do not aspire to live in a Kabul or a Tehran. They genuinely like Beirut's free, open, and pluralist character, and prefer it over the drab insularity of other, more avowedly Islamic cities. Having tasted freedom, the intoxication does not easily wear off. The problem arises when these same Lebanese Muslims, for whatever reasons, lose sight of the *organic* connection that exists between the Beirut they love and the principal reason that it is free and open and generally superior to other Muslim cities: the rooted presence in Beirut—and Lebanon as a whole—of a free, dynamic, industrious, and relatively secure Christian community. In the feverish quest for ways to assert themselves politically, and in the accompanying insensitivity they sometimes exhibit to the existential fears of the Christians, Lebanese Muslims often end up unintentionally undermining the very essence of Beirut they so cherish.

The Islamicization of Lebanon takes many forms, and it can advance surreptitiously or at a galloping pace. In either case the results are not always to the advantage of the inhabitants, Muslims included. Due to prolonged years of war and civil strife, a considerable amount of population segregation has occurred along confessional lines. Mixed areas, both rural and urban, have become fewer as tens of thousands of people found themselves internally displaced. With the cessation of hostilities in recent years some Christians have been slowly trickling back to formerly mixed neighborhoods such as Ras Beirut near the American University, only to find the old haunts sociologically altered.[32] For their part, the Muslims have taken to frequenting the Christian areas on weekends and during holidays in order to partake of the recreational facilities there: cinemas, restaurants, night clubs, mountain resorts, and beaches. These excursions are a welcome escape for many Muslims from the stifling atmosphere of some of their crowded neighborhoods, where strict codes of behavior are observed. In their newly acquired capacity as entertainers, the Christians in fact are reverting back to an old and demeaning role their *dhimmi* ancestors played in the imperial courts of the *caliphate*.

External evidence of growing Islamicization can be seen in the increased incidence of the female headcover, including in some places the Iranian-inspired *chador*. These are more prevalent among the Shi'a, many of whom are fairly recent arrivals in some sections of the city. The enforcement of traditional Islamic dress generates peer pressure that ripples throughout the community, and this in turn has a radicalizing effect that translates into pressures to pray five times a day, fast during Ramadan, and regularly attend Friday prayer services at the local mosque. The middle- and upper-class Sunnis of Beirut, along with certain liberal Shi'a families, do not necessarily support such displays of orthodoxy. In

---

[32] For an interesting and somewhat nostalgic discussion of the shifting sociology of Ras Beirut, see Samir Khalaf, *Lebanon's Predicament* (New York: Columbia University Press, 1987), pp. 261-92.

recent years they have been trying to assume the social, cultural, and educational role they used to share with the Christians in the city before the outbreak of the war and the mass exodus of cultivated foreigners. An attitude of superiority—even of disdain—often pervades these sophisticated Lebanese Muslim urban dwellers, and is directed at the less Westernized Muslims in their midst, who are mentally lumped with "those bearded, turbaned, robed, 'backward' Arabs speaking with unfamiliar accents."[33] Wearing short skirts, drinking whiskey, and dancing in discotheques have become for some the outward manifestations of a new, superficial sociological affinity with the Christians—a new "Lebanese-ness" having little to do with deeper shared values (if indeed such values exist) or a common attachment to the land.

Finally, a word about the Druze community, a heterodox offshoot of Islam dating back to the eleventh century and featuring Neoplatonic and other esoteric elements, including *taqiyya*. The Druze historically competed with the Maronites in their attachment to Mount Lebanon, where they had sought refuge from persecution. Their paramount concern became survival, and their strategy was to ally themselves staunchly with a dominant or strong party or community, whoever that might be at any given point in time. They developed a perennial rivalry with the Maronites that at times reached the point of bloody clashes. They have traditionally divided into two broad tendencies: one intransigent and confrontational and the other flexible and conciliatory. The former tendency is currently dominated by the Jumblat family; the Arslans represent the latter. Depending on which way the political winds are blowing, each tendency comes to the fore or retreats to the sidelines of the Lebanese political arena with clockwork precision. With the end of the war in Lebanon, the Druze found themselves effectively controlling their own little canton in the Shuf mountains and adjoining areas of central Lebanon.[34]

CONDITIONS IN POST-TAIF LEBANON

As a composite society, Lebanon exhibits a range of perceptions, counterperceptions, and misperceptions exchanged among its various religious communities. Whereas other states in the region are increasingly involved in sorting out their relations with one another within a new and gradually emerging regime of regional peace, Lebanon continues to focus on problems not only of reconstitution, but literally of redefinition.

Implicitly, there are many Lebanons, a multiplicity of "Lebanons-in-the-making," and dreams of future Lebanons, which—depending on which community one listens to—range along the continuum between the two

---

[33] A phrase used by an elderly Sunni Muslim from a well-known family in Beirut.

[34] For a concise survey of the Druze community and its beliefs, see Robert Brenton Betts, *The Druze* (New Haven, CT: Yale University Press, 1988).

improbable extremes of an Islamic republic and a Christian state. Any dissection of Lebanon's polity can easily amount to an anatomy of incompatible, if not antagonistic, communal agendas which underscores a basic truth: while Lebanon's sub-national communal entities endure, its supra-national political arrangements are ephemeral.

Nevertheless, Lebanon is not fated to remain in a perpetual state of fragmentation. In fact, it seems to go through cycles in which the heterogeneous sub-national mosaic congeals into a streamlined national structure through a process of consensus and compromise, often encouraged by external forces but resting upon well-defined internal components, only to experience eventual collapse and disintegration at times of acute crises or "moments of truth"[35] and revert back to its original sub-national (i.e., communal) aggregates. Then the entire process commences all over again.

These cycles are a reflection of a uniquely Lebanese political dialectic that manifests itself under a variety of headings: unity/fragmentation, Muslim/Christian, sectarian/secular, Arab/Lebanese, city/mountain, sub-national/supra-communal, center/periphery, compromise/confrontation, and others. The peculiar Lebanese political idiom is therefore inherently dichotomous, and a constant underlying tension—a dialectical interplay between extremes—informs all political discourse and developments in Lebanon. Yet the Lebanese pattern of employing temporary "solutions" in the name of political compromise can be a double-edged sword. On one hand, it bespeaks an admirable Lebanese resilience in the face of prolonged battering and terrific odds. On the other, however, it tends to accelerate the cycle of coalescence and collapse by masking chronic incompatibilities and glossing over residual antagonisms.

Despite the presence in Lebanon of endemic communal cleavages, a genuine desire for peaceful coexistence surfaces regularly; it is often prompted by a combination of external pressure and internal mercantile considerations and imperatives, however, rather than a unified and articulated national ethos. Although there is nothing wrong with the commercial enterprise and entrepreneurial success that so many Lebanese display, this cannot constitute the sole or even overriding basis for lasting communal coexistence. Without at least a modicum of shared values and aspirations to supplement mercantile advantage—and a corresponding set of reliable, institutionally enshrined legal and constitutional safeguards to guarantee these values and minimize the impact of deleterious external meddling—any state or national arrangement that emerges will always remain fundamentally flimsy.

The Lebanon of peaceful coexistence between Muslims and Christians has been portrayed romantically as "a bird with two wings," with each community representing a wing. The obvious implication is that the bird

---

[35] Hourani, "Lebanon From Feudalism to Nation-State," in *The Emergence of the Modern Middle East*, p. 143.

cannot fly with one wing alone and needs both to function. If any deeper values and assumptions bind the two communities together, however, they remain largely unformulated beyond vague poetic imagery laden with nostalgia. Such coexistence entails creative communal interaction that preserves the integrity of each sub-national group while providing a framework for nation-building on the basis of mutual respect for freedom, pluralism, openness, and basic rights. Moreover, for peaceful coexistence between two groups harboring unequal levels of fear to succeed, the party with lesser anxieties (in this case, the Muslims) needs to constantly reassure the existentially fearful party (the Christians), and their reassurances must be credible—namely, authenticated by actual deeds. The onus of successful coexistence conducive to lasting contentment therefore lies on the shoulders of the least frightened community. The reality of captive Lebanon tells a different story.

Divided societies can be precariously "at peace" with themselves even when their constituent components are merely living side-by-side, hardly interacting beyond the bare economic necessities. But when such divided societies are additionally saddled with foreign occupation, and when the presence of the occupier encourages some members of a particular community to believe that they are at an advantage over the other communities, a potentially lethal process of irreversible transformation detrimental to freedom is set in motion. Lebanon currently finds itself in such a sad state. About 10 percent of its territory is under Israeli control, and the remaining 90 percent is subject to direct Syrian military occupation and indirect Syrian political control. The accepted "wisdom" in international circles appears to be that Lebanon, for whatever reasons, continues to require this open-ended, dual "overlordship" by its two neighbors—certainly the 90 percent of it under Syrian hegemony.

Should this abnormal state of affairs persist indefinitely, however, much that is of value to Lebanon and the region as a whole is in danger of being irretrievably lost. As the twenty-first century approaches, Lebanon displays many odd anachronisms, not least its vestiges of religious and clan feudalism. But the Middle East is itself rife with even less appealing anachronisms: various Islamic fundamentalisms, generally closed societies under repressive Arab governments, economic stagnation and squandering of resources, illiteracy and parochialism, the *bedouin* mentality and desert culture of Arabia, and the deplorable state of Arab women are but a few prominent examples.

To speak of Lebanon's unique experience of freedom in the middle decades of this century is not to appeal to a contrived mystique or promote some form of mythical self-glorification. A careful scrutiny of Lebanon's pre-1975 history would reveal a set of indicators of freedom—the fruits of a genuinely liberal, pluralist, and open society in the Middle Eastern context—that, despite being couched at times in romantic clichés, rest on a solid kernel of objective, verifiable truth. Examples include the most independent press in the Arab world; prolific publishing without censorship; thriving national sectors such as education, medicine, banking, entertainment, services, and tourism; free trade; a plethora of political parties and fora operating openly; and much more. In spite of the occasional blemishes and imperfections that marred the actual manifestations of these freedoms, Lebanon was fully justified in claiming to be the freest society in the Arab world. Moreover, Lebanon's pre-war economic prosperity was never the exclusive privilege of any single religious group, but had a generalized "trickle down" effect that belied such stereotypical—and erroneous—descriptions of pre-war Lebanon as the land of the "haves" (i.e., rich Christians) and "have nots" (poor Muslims), where the former basked in *la dolce vita* while the latter toiled away in misery.

The prerequisite for understanding Lebanon is an appreciation of its nuances, rather than the oft-peddled stereotypes. For example, Lebanon never fit the late Elie Kedourie's blanket description of Middle Eastern regimes: "Traditional rule in the Middle East may be characterized as Oriental despotism in which . . . the state is stronger than society."[36] In fact, the precise opposite has always been true about Lebanon—society, not the state, is consistently the stronger and more durable of the two. Similarly, it is not necessarily the case, as Kedourie asserts, that constitutional representative government works only in a secular context.[37] This may be true in regard to the Western experience, but Lebanon's idiosyncratic multi-confessional version of consociational democracy among religious communities, in which distinctive subgroups are preserved within a system of proportional representation, offers an example of representative democracy among a plurality of religious or sectarian units.[38]

The pressing question in post-Taif Lebanon is not so much how Christians and Muslims can live together, nor even how one reconciles the Christian and Muslim conceptions of Lebanon, but rather how to protect basic rights and freedoms for individuals and communities regardless of their religious affiliation from the mounting ravages of prolonged

---

[36] See Elie Kedourie, *Democracy and Arab Political Culture* (Washington, DC: Washington Institute for Near East Policy, 1992), p. 8. In his section on Lebanon (pp. 47-61), Kedourie unfortunately echoes some of the distorting stereotypes. He speaks without qualification, for example, about "wealthy" Maronites and "less well off" Muslims (p. 60) and concludes from Lebanon's recurring crises and some dubious data on the growth of the Shi'a community that parliamentary government is no longer possible there (pp. 56, 61).

[37] Ibid., pp. 95-96. Elsewhere, Kedourie is actually more appreciative of Lebanon's nuances: "It may therefore be said that the autonomous province of Mount Lebanon was the only area of the Middle East in which, for a few decades [i.e., 1861–1915], there existed a regime recognizably constitutional and representative" (p. 50).

[38] It is lamentable that, in the wake of the Gulf War, so much was written about the possibilities of democratizing the Middle East without a single mention of Lebanon; the carnage of recent years has all but obscured its significance in the region. The ink on the sensitive subject of democracy abruptly stopped flowing when it was realized that too much freedom could destabilize the oil-rich dynasties of Arabia; in the *realpolitik* world of wealth and power, values are inevitably subordinate to expediency.

foreign—and specifically Syrian—occupation. The Lebanon war has not really ended. Though the guns are silent and security has improved on some levels, a heavy price is being exacted for these modest normalizing steps in the form of a tighter noose around freedoms and a steady erosion of Lebanon's distinctive characteristics. The war therefore has merely assumed a different form, with subtle new demarcation lines separating the two warring sides. The decisive confrontation for the foreseeable future is between Lebanon's beleaguered civil society in all its aspects (which often traverse religious divides) and the relentless hegemonic onslaught on this civil society by the Damascus regime. Thus, after years of bloody internecine strife fueled by outside interference, the Lebanon war has metamorphosed into a showdown pitting Syria and its local proxies against the vast majority of the Lebanese population.

Assuming that Lebanon is Syria's "near abroad" (to borrow an expression from the Russian geopolitical context), this is apparently sufficient reason in the eyes of Syria's ruling Ba'th party to render the definition of its "vital interests" in Lebanon as elastic and open-ended. Since the November 1989 Taif agreement, Syria has been allowed to get away with a number of steps in Lebanon that have underscored the open-endedness in its influence there. The agreement has been only partially implemented: provisions requiring Syrian redeployment to the Bekaa Valley have been ignored, while wide-ranging measures have been taken to bolster the so-called "privileged relationship" between the two countries. In other words, since its inception Taif has been methodically Syrianized and augmented by a string of "bilateral agreements" designed to lead toward the gradual merger of Lebanon with Syria at all levels.

In October 1990, the United States and Israel looked the other way while the Syrian army and air force effectively routed the forces of General Michel Aoun, the only remaining pocket of resistance to Syria's takeover of Lebanon. During the 1991 Gulf War, President Assad provided the "fig leaf" of token support from a reputedly radical Arab state to the U.S.-led anti-Iraq coalition. His reward was continued freedom of action in Lebanon. By the time the Madrid peace conference convened later that year and launched the current Middle East peace process, Syria had become firmly entrenched in Lebanon and was vigorously consolidating its visible as well as covert presence there. Since Madrid there has been a marked reluctance on the part of either the United States or Israel to challenge Syria's stranglehold over Lebanon, for fear of jeopardizing an eventual peace deal between Syria and Israel.

The Taif agreement initiated a steady process of erosion on more than one level in Lebanon. War-weariness resulting in a kind of inertia in the population provided ideal conditions for this erosion, and a convenient facade for the occupation to entrench itself. As the peace process slowly inches forward and the intertwined Syrian and Lebanese tracks stagnate, drift in Lebanon is turning into an imperceptible slide toward a set of irreversible "facts on the ground" intended to promote outright assimilation with Syria; the *de facto* occupation is gradually becoming *de jure* annexation. Instead of recognizing and accommodating Lebanon's internal socio-cultural heterogeneity and potentially creative multicultural face, the goal of forced assimilation and homogenization on every level leading to a colorless monoculturalism is being advanced in the name of "national reconciliation" and "national reintegration," and in the ultimate service of Syrian purposes and Ba'th expansionist ideology.

    The Taif agreement (also referred to as the National Conciliation Document) inaugurated this homogenizing assimilative trend, and the Syrian-appointed regime in Beirut has been reinforcing and accelerating it ever since. Instead of serving as a basis for national reconciliation (as it was initially trumpeted by its supporters), Taif has aggravated latent Christian fears without really satisfying the other communities. In other words, it completely ignored the existing asymmetry between the existential fears and the socio-political grievances of the two main communal subgroups in the Lebanese polity. The Syrianized Taif in fact went further by undermining what remained of Christian political influence without fulfilling the aspirations of Lebanon's Muslim political establishment. By curtailing the powers of the presidency—a post traditionally reserved for a Maronite Christian—and rendering it largely ceremonial, and seemingly enhancing the standing of the Sunni prime minister and Shi'a speaker of parliament, Taif set the stage for infighting and paralysis among the three key posts referred to euphemistically as the *troika*. Naturally, at times of disagreement and deadlock, the only place to turn for a quick resolution of the impasse is Damascus. The Beirut-Damascus highway has witnessed a brisk two-way traffic by an assortment of Lebanese politicians traveling to Syria seeking favor or attempting to shore up sagging political fortunes. In the "virtual state" of post-Taif Lebanon, where the "government" exists only in the minds of its officials, and all communities are undergoing a regimen of domestication, Syria is the maestro and true beneficiary.[39]

---

[39] For a critical appraisal of the Taif document (and particularly its impact on human rights and Lebanese sovereignty), see *Muqarrarat At-Ta'if wa Huquq Al-Insan* (*The Taif Accords and Human Rights*), (Beirut: Foundation for Human and Humanitarian Rights, December 1989). On the Taif process and its consequences, see also Habib Malik, "Lebanon in the 1990s: Stability Without Freedom?" in *Global Affairs* 7, no. 1 (Winter 1992), pp. 84-91.

II

The Evaporation of Politics

Politics in Lebanon currently lie in a comatose state.[1] Normal political life—where governments come to power through accepted channels of selection backed by popular approval, and an opposition is able to exist and freely attempt through prescribed constitutional channels to replace the existing government—with which Lebanon used to be acquainted is utterly missing in the post-Taif era. Responsible nonconformity has all but vanished and pervading intimidation has become the norm—as evidenced by the total absence of effective and independent political parties democratically competing for power.[2]

Though many of the political parties in pre-1975 Lebanon were differentiated by broad ideological categories (within a localized Lebanese context) such as Christian-liberal, Arabist, socialist, leftist, pan-Syrian, traditionalist, opportunist, and romantic-nationalist, they were little more than family-run sectarian groups with strong clan loyalties and deep feudal roots[3]—usually revolving around charismatic figures or clan leaders with familiar names such as Gemayel, Chamoun, Franjieh, Jumblat, Antoun Saadeh, and Adnan Hakim—and lacked adequate institutional structures capable of effectively outlasting their founder or his dynasty. Despite these shortcomings—and the fact that competition among them generally fell short of strict Western standards of democracy—they managed to put forward political programs on a number of important issues and often attracted wide followings. Their mode of interaction was a clear indicator

---

[1] See Farid El-Khazen, "Al-Nizam Al-Intikhabi Al-Lubnani," *al-Nahar*, October 14, 1995.

[2] In 1991, four political parties (including the pro-Iraq Arab Socialist Ba'th party) were dissolved on orders from the minister of the interior. In spring 1994, the Lebanese Forces party, the political arm of the Christian militia, was dissolved following an explosion at a church in the coastal city of Jounieh in which the militia was allegedly implicated.

[3] "Familism" is a term coined apparently by Samir Khalaf to describe the peculiarities of the Lebanese political scene; see the chapter entitled "Changing Forms of Political Patronage" in *Lebanon's Predicament*, especially pp. 88-92. See also pp. 230-34 on familism, pp. 102-20 on primordial loyalties, pp. 146-60 on nepotism and paternalism, and pp. 161-84 on family associations. On the power of the family, Khalaf writes (p. 97): "The ascriptive ties of family solidarity and communal loyalties have for a long time provided the only trustable and meaningful basis for integrating the social order. Any other form of collaboration, particularly if it is sustained by the rational instruments of a nation-state—i.e., anonymous large-scale organizations such as political parties, civil bureaucracies or class loyalties—have not had an enthusiastic reception in Lebanon. Indeed, in some instances, they have proved disastrous and too disruptive."

of the considerable degree of political freedom in Lebanon at the time. In a political sense, Lebanon was the Italy of the Middle East, with all its anarchic politics and corrupt politicians. In Middle Eastern terms, it was a breath of fresh air in a region where freedom has been a rare commodity.

During the war years, many of Lebanon's political parties degenerated into paramilitary militias, and when the fighting ended they faced insurmountable obstacles to reconstituting themselves in ways that would allow them to retain a dwindling base of support and offset the prevailing disillusionment among the youth. Rifts emerged and widened in the various communities between the pragmatically self-aggrandizing political elites and their traditional grassroots supporters. No longer were the customary compromises and bargains at the top sufficient to forge lasting links with the rank-and-file below. In the absence of independent elites whose political responsibility was based solely on merit, the demise of the traditional family-based parties during and after the war years—either as a result of death or intervention by foreign actors—created a serious leadership crisis and represented a political vacuum in Lebanon.[4] The stifling constraints of Syrian hegemony currently preclude any of the declining political parties from reassembling themselves and broadening their constituencies, and similarly prevent new political parties with any semblance of independent thinking and initiative from arising.

Lebanon's politics declined further as it tried to wrestle with Taif's legacy of constitutional tampering. With Syria the real powerbroker in Lebanon, ominous provisions giving the government the right to conclude treaties without informing parliament or publicizing the texts in advance have served to consolidate control from Damascus. Armed with this constitutional amendment, the Syrians hastened to impose a series of bilateral agreements on the Lebanese government that can be characterized only as steps toward creeping annexation or absorption by stealth. Nowhere has the decline of Lebanese politics been more evident, however, than in parliamentary and presidential elections. In adjusting the proportional representation of Christians and Muslims in parliament to conform to a 50-50 ratio, Taif increased the number of representatives beyond the traditional ninety-nine and called for the "appointment" of new members to the chamber to replace deceased ones and reach the required number. The dangerous precedent of appointing (rather than electing) supposed representatives of the people violates the essence of parliamentary democracy and departs radically from Lebanese political norms.

In 1992, the government (with Syrian approval) saw fit to call general parliamentary elections despite a strong wave of opposition protesting the timing of such elections and insisting on international supervision to

---

[4] On the details of the shifting fortunes of Lebanon's political elites during the war, see Farid El-Khazen, "The Making and Unmaking of Lebanon's Political Elites from Independence to Taif," *Beirut Review* (Fall 1993), especially pp. 58-60. For background, see also Khalaf, *Lebanon's Predicament*, pp. 121-45.

ensure the elections were free and fair. The opposition enjoyed a wide popular following and centered mainly on the alienated Christians, along with significant disgruntled segments from the other communities. The impressive extent of this opposition notwithstanding, the government proceeded with preparations for the elections by passing a highly controversial electoral law that re-drew the electoral districts in such a way as to ensure the outcome of elections beforehand. The uneven re-districting affected both the size and configuration of the districts and created "hostage" candidates—namely, candidates of one religious confession forced to run in districts with a majority of voters of another religious affiliation. Most of the "hostage" candidates were Christian. Moreover, the electoral law was passed very close to the date of elections, leaving little room for the candidates to campaign meaningfully.

Taif had used the *muhafaza* (large territorial and administrative unit) as the basis for subdividing electoral districts. The rationale was that larger units promote national unity because they contain a greater confessional mix than smaller, more segregated districts. This might work in a country free of foreign occupation where reasonably autonomous political parties could compete in a democratic spirit, but that is hardly the case in Lebanon. Under the current realities, large electoral districts would inevitably fall prey to the manipulation of external influence. Thus, the 1992 electoral law not only perverted the Taif principle of large electoral districts, it produced a political landscape tailor-made to guarantee an outcome favorable to Syrian wishes. Not content merely to manipulate the *muhafazas*, the Syrians flagrantly attempted to "fix" the elections in advance through the electoral law and their Lebanese proxies. Their local apologists then tried to justify this blatant interference by arguing insipidly that outside powers had always influenced parliamentary and presidential elections in Lebanon in the past, implying that Syrian intervention was nothing new. In fact, this argument obfuscated precisely the unprecedented and highly alarming level of heavy-handed manipulation and tampering in every facet of Lebanese civil and political life by Syria and its local Lebanese agents.[5]

---

[5] For a thorough appraisal of Lebanon's 1992 parliamentary elections and their many anomalies (as well as comparisons with parliamentary elections prior to 1975), see Farid El-Khazen, "Al-intikhabat Al-niyabiyya Al-'ula fi Lubnan ma ba'd Al-Harb: 'Matarees' Ad-dimukratiyya Al-jadida (The First Parliamentary Elections in Post-War Lebanon: Barricades of the New Democracy)" in *Al-intikhabat Al-'ula fi Lubnan ma ba'd Al-Harb: Al-arqam wal Waqa'ih wa Dalalat (The First Elections in Post-War Lebanon: Statistics, Facts, Indicators)*, eds. Farid El-Khazen and Paul Salem (Beirut: Lebanese Center for Policy Studies, 1993), pp. 29-116. See also El-Khazen, "Lebanon's First Post-War Parliamentary Elections–1992," *Middle East Policy* 3, no. 1 (1994), pp. 120-36. In both studies, El-Khazen makes abundantly clear that in the post-Taif era of Syrian domination, there has been an unprecedented qualitative decline that renders previous external interventions and internal irregularities (what Kedourie calls the "ingenious gerrymandering" of the 1950s and 1960s) innocuous by comparison; see Kedourie, *Democracy and Arab Political Culture* (Washington, DC: Washington Institute for Near East Policy, 1992), pp. 58-59.

Christian opposition to the 1992 parliamentary elections turned into a general boycott by roughly 87 percent of Christians and other eligible voters. This represented a popular rejection of the "rubber stamp" parliament Syria was in the process of engineering. Nevertheless, the elections went ahead and thereafter a palpable mood of national demoralization and gloom descended on the population—and principally the Christians, thus deepening their existing alienation into a prolonged political sulk. Thereafter, Christian opposition leaders and the bulk of their constituents expressed their displeasure by avoiding as much as possible any entanglement in politics conducted according to Syrian dictates. The 1992 parliamentary elections violated the principles of representative democracy, deepened communal polarization, coalesced the political alienation of the Christians, and eliminated any remaining chances for engaging in a semblance of normal politics in Lebanon.[6]

If the 1992 elections were highly problematic by any objective standard, the repeat of the exercise four years later represented an even smoother display of Syrian choreography. The new electoral law for the 1996 parliamentary elections—once again promulgated only weeks before the actual voting—turned out to be more conspicuously Syrian-serving than its predecessor. It relied on a carefully crafted mixture of the *muhafaza* and a smaller administrative district, the *qada'*, to ensure maximum compliance with Syrian desires. The process required a local *chef d'orchestre*, and Minister of Interior Michel Murr fit the part nicely. He made sure large numbers of recently naturalized Syrians voted for the Syrian-favored candidates, and his thugs applied all sorts of pressure on government employees, civil servants, and ordinary citizens to do the same. Extensive manipulation of voter turnout percentages and other voting-related statistics also took place.

But Syrian meddling did not end there. Damascus intervened directly in the last two rounds of voting in South Lebanon and the Bekaa Valley in order to hastily assemble a Shi'a coalition composed of militant Hezbollah and their more moderate rival, Amal (headed by Speaker of Parliament Nabih Berri), in order to rescue Hezbollah from further humiliation after their poor showing in the first three rounds of the elections. The Syrian strategy worked, thus thwarting the efforts of the Beirut authorities, principally Prime Minister Hariri, to weaken the Hezbollah.

Although Christian voter turnout was low—particularly in Beirut, the south, and the Bekaa—it did not approach the overwhelming 1992 election boycott. This was due primarily to lingering internal discord among Christian opposition leaders both in Lebanon and in exile abroad. In addition, a certain logic of politics on the local level, particularly in

---

[6] See Farid El-Khazen, "The Making and Unmaking of Lebanon's Political Elites from Independence to Taif," pp. 61-64. As El-Khazen puts it (p. 62), "The 1992 parliamentary elections ... produced the least representative parliament since independence, had the lowest voter turnout, and brought to office the largest number of unopposed candidates in the history of Lebanon's parliamentary elections."

semi-feudal societies where the rule of law is largely absent, often dictates that voters and candidates temporarily subordinate ideological considerations and positions of principle to mundane necessities such as securing government services and largesse for the community, promoting family chances at political participation, and demonstrating loyalty to clans and their prominent personalities.[7]

In addition to the many irregularities associated with them, the two anomalous elections of 1992 and 1996 paved the way for further assaults on the sanctity of a critical document in Lebanese politics: the constitution. From its inception in 1926, the Lebanese constitution has been amended eight times. Never before Taif, however, was it done so callously and cavalierly. Taif opened up a Pandora's Box of notorious precedents, and the country has been descending down the slippery slope of constitutional tinkering ever since.

In the fall of 1995, the summer-long speculation about Lebanon's presidential elections was suddenly put to an end in the most contemptuous manner when the government (with the appropriate nod from Damascus) amended Article 49 of the constitution—which limits the president's term in office—to extend the term from six years to nine years. Then, in similar mechanical fashion, the Lebanese parliament convened to approve the amendment and voted to extend the tenure of current pro-Syrian president Elias Hrawi by three years. This cynical blow to what was left of Lebanese sovereignty resulted from Syria's desire to freeze the status quo and put everything in Lebanon "on hold" pending further developments in its stalled peace negotiations with Israel. Under the *pax Syriana*, nothing—including the constitution—is sacrosanct any longer in Lebanon. Taif effectively castrated the Lebanese presidency, rendering the occupant a pathetic figurehead; with the amendment of Article 49, nothing less than the cancellation of the Lebanese state—or what was left of it—occurred amidst an atmosphere of tangible intimidation.

SYRIAN-IMPOSED BILATERAL AGREEMENTS

One noteworthy feature of Lebanese civil society is an emerging populism that manifested itself throughout 1989–90 in the form of a

---

[7] For more discussion of the 1996 parliamentary elections, see Habib Malik "Parliamentary Elections in Lebanon: An Early Assessment," *PolicyWatch* no. 216 (September 6, 1996); and "Parliamentary Elections in Lebanon: A Final Assessment," *PolicyWatch* no. 221 (October 4, 1996), Washington Institute for Near East Policy. On the relative benefits and liabilities of large electoral districts, particularly relating to the 1996 parliamentary elections, see Farid El-Khazen: "Al-Nizam Al-intikhabi fi Wadha'ifihi wa Mafa'ilihi As-Siyasiyya," *al-Nahar*, October 13, 1995; and "Al-Nizam Al-intikhabi fi Lubnan," *al-Nahar*, October 14, 1995. For an early anticipation of the new electoral law and 1996 parliamentary elections, see "Carving the Parliamentary Cake: Lebanon and a New Election Law," *Lebanon Report*, no. 3 (Fall 1995), pp. 26-29; and Ghassan Moukheiber, "Selected Issues in a New Lebanese Electoral Law," ibid., pp. 30-35.

spontaneous outpouring of patriotic protest against Syrian occupation. Christian political sullenness and the general boycott of the 1992 parliamentary elections both resulted directly or indirectly from this populist awakening. Lebanon's populist tradition has roots going back at least to the nineteenth century when it existed among the Christians as a mountain populism directed usually against the excesses of Ottoman rule. As in those earlier days, the populist defiance of foreign pressure in 1989 required a figure around whom to rally and found one in the charismatic—and somewhat erratic—commander-in-chief of the Lebanese army, General Michel Aoun. The anti-Syrian populism associated with the Aoun phenomenon was not confined to the Christians, spilling over significantly into other communities, mainly the Shi'a. Whatever untainted opposition to Syrian domination currently exists in Lebanon derives mainly from the Aoun-inspired popular current and includes some prominent political personalities who opposed the Taif process.[8]

Populism alone is not enough to dislodge foreign domination, however, particularly if the former remains fluid and unstructured and lacks proper institutional points of reference. Lebanon's patriotic surge has at times been too diffuse and ambiguous to be effective. Its key inspirational leader, Gen. Aoun, has been in exile for over six years and his reading of regional and international politics is often woefully deficient.[9] The populist groundswell is characterized by a variety of internal strands which are not always in harmony with one another, often resulting in divisiveness and lack of coordination. As with every example of populist display, the calmer voices of intellectuals and theoreticians are invariably drowned in a sea of genuine passion and emotional outpouring. Unlike a tightly knit political party, sustained planning for contingencies in the context of an amorphous populist movement is very difficult, no matter how well-meaning and authentic it might be.

Despite the severe limitations of raw populism, however, it has had some tangible beneficial effects in staving off or at least slowing down Lebanon's absorption by Syria. Though disorganized, the mass of people opposed to Syrian hegemony have acted as a solid, inert bulwark against assimilation. Their mere existence and conscious rejection of "Syrianization" allows them to resist absorption and even hamper attempts at neutralization. Syria may have subjugated "official" Lebanon and made significant strides in intimidation and domestication in other areas; but Lebanon's battered yet still pulsating civil society is evidence that

---

[8] The list of opposition leaders includes prominent Christian figures Gen. Michel Aoun, Raymond Edde (in exile in Paris), Dory Chamoun (National Liberal Party), and Maronite Patriarch Nasrallah Sfeir. Other opponents of the status quo (though essentially political opportunists) include Albert Moukhaiber (Greek Orthodox former member of parliament), Hussein Husseini (Shi'a former speaker of parliament), Omar Karami (Sunni former prime minister), and Najah Wakim (Greek Orthodox member of parliament).

[9] For a candid summary of the views of Gen. Aoun, see "Michel Aoun: If Lebanon Fails, So Does the Middle East," *Middle East Quarterly* 2, no. 4 (December 1995), pp. 59-66.

Damascus still has a long way to go in these efforts. Aware of this obstacle, the Syrians and their surrogates in the Beirut government have been trying to create the impression that the latter does indeed enjoy popular support. The local media accord maximum coverage to public appearances by officials, and in the days following the forced extension of Hrawi's tenure in office, displays were staged for the cameras of "popular" delegations flocking to the presidential palace from all around the country to offer their congratulations. The artificial and contrived nature of these attempts, however, was lost on very few among the Lebanese.

But perhaps the Syrians' greatest success against this latent populist hostility has been in fragmenting the opposition, which in turn led to the dissolution of the elections boycott in summer 1996. Those "opposition" candidates who did finally win remain securely within the Syrian orbit on all vital matters, both Lebanese and regional. In an attempt to provide a deceptive appearance of democratic debate, the Beirut government's propagandists have gone out of their way since the parliamentary elections to portray this fabricated and ultimately captive opposition inside the legislative assembly as the "true" opposition, supplanting the leaders of the boycott.

Despite these efforts, however, Syria's chief handicap in Lebanon remains its near-universal lack of admirers across Lebanon's communal spectrum. In fact, resentment among Muslims has at times been greater than among Christians, simply because on a day-to-day basis the Syrian presence in Muslim areas has been much more intrusive and invasive. The difference is that the Muslims have tended to be far less vocal about their real sentiments regarding Syrian occupation than their Christian counterparts. The lack of existential urgency in Muslim fears, combined with a high level of intimidation (the anticipation that Syrian retribution would be swift and brutal), generally mutes Muslim complaints. Beyond Syria's high-profile operatives in the Lebanese government and those in the Muslim community who instinctively turn to outside regional support to prevent a resurgence of Christian prominence, there is little genuine affection for Syria in Lebanon. In short, Syria's allies in Lebanon are in a decided minority.

Taming Lebanese civil society was initially a daunting task for the Syrians. The nature of the Assad regime and the absence of a vibrant civil society inside Syria itself did not help the authorities in Damascus to grasp adequately the convoluted intricacies of Lebanese society. Though adept at "divide and rule" tactics and displaying a remarkable ability to play various Lebanese factions against one another, the Syrians required a more subtle and incremental approach to achieve their goal of the eventual total annexation and assimilation of Lebanon. History shows that complex, multi-communal societies with extended experience of free expression and demonstrated entrepreneurial initiative—no matter how beleaguered— outlast totalitarian, hegemonic regimes possessing antiquated militaries and vestiges of an obsolete command economy, no matter how seemingly stable and secure these regimes may be at any given time. Perhaps the best contemporary analogy was Eastern Europe under Soviet domination: If Ba'thist Syria represents the last Brezhnev state, Lebanon is the last "captive nation," resembling the countries of East Europe and the Baltic in the 1980s.[10]

Yet Syria's domination and absorption of Lebanon is a problem not of the state (except incidentally), but rather an urgent problem of the community and the individual. It is in the schools, trade and labor unions, professional associations and syndicates, student groups, non-governmental organizations, ecclesiastical institutions, and a variety of similar local bodies (not to mention countless households) that ongoing resistance is taking place—often quite impressively. Once again, these fronts of resistance are not confined to any single religious community in the country, although clearly a Lebanon without free Christians would quickly turn into a version of Syria. This has not yet happened, but Syrian-dominated Lebanon is in many respects becoming increasingly frightening precisely because the Syrians are learning to practice incremental absorption with increasing skill.

From the start, the Syrians sought to buttress their military and political control over Lebanon by imposing a string of special bilateral "agreements" on the Beirut government. They forced these so-called agreements through the Lebanese executive branch and parliament, in part as a compensation for not being able to fully penetrate and transform Lebanese civil society into something more pliable. In fact, the general public knew nothing of these agreements until they were published in local newspapers, by which time they had become *faits accomplis*. The ultimate intention behind these agreements is nothing short of complete merger between Lebanon and Syria on a number of vital levels—the forced legislation of Lebanon's full absorption by Syria.

In 1990 and early 1991 the Syrians conducted some preliminary explorations of fertile areas for bilateral agreements. Visits by hand-picked Lebanese delegations to Damascus resulted in the rudiments of a trade deal and media cooperation between the two countries.[11] In late 1990, the London-based pan-Arab daily *al-Hayat* ran a lengthy article reviewing Lebanese-Syrian economic relations since their independence and emphasizing the historical intimacy of these relations. The article concluded that despite the obvious difference in the economic systems of the two states (Lebanese free enterprise vs. Syrian centralized socialism),

---

[10] The analogy was first made by David Wurmser at a seminar at the Washington Institute for Near East Policy, on May 17, 1995. Daniel Pipes later observed that gradual Syrian demographic and socio-cultural meddling in Lebanon is reminiscent of what the Soviets did to transform the Baltic states in sociologically sensitive areas such as population transfers and education. An important qualification in Lebanon's favor, however, is that unlike many of the East European states, Lebanon excelled in free enterprise long before Syrian occupation and continues to do so even under the strains of Syrian control.

[11] See *al-Nahar*, October 26, 1990; and *al-Liwa'*, November 20, 1990.

there was room for close cooperation leading eventually to integration.[12] In February 1991 trade negotiations between Lebanon and Syria resulted in draft agreements on overland transportation and customs duties at the borders,[13] and by March a joint Lebanese-Syrian committee had produced the outlines of an agreement for agricultural cooperation.[14]

In May 1991 came the "bombshell" announcement that Lebanon and Syria were going to sign a "Treaty of Brotherhood, Cooperation, and Coordination between the Lebanese Republic and the Syrian Arab Republic" in Damascus. The treaty was signed amid audible protests from Christian leaders, principally Maronite Patriarch Nasrallah Sfeir, exiled Gen. Aoun, and token American and French "warnings" about Lebanon "falling under Syrian control."[15] Initial Israeli reactions were mixed, with one official view being that the treaty made Syria directly responsible in the eyes of the world for security on the Israeli-Lebanese border, and therefore it would now be in Syria's interest for the border to become quiet like the Golan Heights had been for years. This proved to be an erroneous assessment based on wishful thinking, as recurrent flare-ups have shown.[16]

The language of the "Treaty of Brotherhood" contains ideological expressions intended to bolster the Ba'th claim of the "privileged brotherly ties" and "oneness" of the two states and their peoples. According to the preamble, for example, common historical roots, shared interests, and an intertwined destiny define and distinguish the special relationship between Syria and Lebanon. These vital organic links in turn pave the way for "the highest levels of cooperation and coordination between the two states in the political, economic, security, cultural, scientific, and other areas."[17] The treaty mentions a range of agreements it presages and which are slated to follow in its wake—on economics, agriculture, industry, commerce, transportation, communications, and customs—along with future joint projects and coordinated development schemes. It also stresses that neither country should at any time become a source of security threats to the other, specifically stating that "Lebanon ought under no circumstances to allow itself to become a passageway or a haven for any power or state or organization aiming to undermine its, or Syria's, security."

The treaty further stipulates that, following the full implementation of "political reforms" outlined in the Taif agreement, the two governments will jointly decide on the redeployment of Syrian forces to the Bekaa and other locations, the precise size of these forces, and their relationship with

---

[12] See Marwan Abdullah, "Al-'alaqat Al-iktisadiyya Al-lubnaniyya-Al-suriyya fi dhil Itifaq at-Taif," (Lebanese-Syrian Economic Relations in the Shadow of the Taif Agreement) in *al-Hayat*, December 27, 1990.

[13] *Al-Safir*, February 13, 1991.

[14] *Al-Nahar*, March 28, 1991.

[15] See *al-Hayat*, May 21, 1991; and *al-Nahar*, May 22, 1991.

[16] See *Ha'aretz*, May 22, 1991; see also *al-Nahar*, May 23, 1991.

[17] For the full Arabic text of the treaty, see *al-Nahar*, May 23, 1991.

Lebanese authorities. In addition, there is a clause stating that Lebanon and Syria are both Arab countries that are members of the Arab League, the United Nations, and the Non-Aligned Movement, and as such must closely coordinate their foreign policies to reflect "the shared destiny and interests of the two countries." Finally, in a disturbing bid for greater institutional integration, the treaty creates a Higher Council composed of the leaders of the two countries, and a number of satellite committees intended to shepherd a gradual and comprehensive strategy of merger. There is a Follow-up and Coordination Committee, a Foreign Affairs Committee, a Committee for Economic and Social Affairs, and a Defense and Security Committee. The specific tasks of each are clearly spelled out in the body of the treaty.[18]

Aside from continued grumblings by the Maronite Patriarch, some demonstrations by Lebanese expatriates and exiles in Paris, and a U.S. rhetorical resolve to "follow closely" the implementation of the Syrian-Lebanese treaty, the international community hardly took notice of how firmly ensconced Lebanon had become in the Syrian sphere of influence.[19] With the "Treaty of Brotherhood" serving as the baseline and point of reference the Syrians intended, the floodgates of "special agreements" were opened. First came the August 1991 "Defense and Security Agreement Between Lebanon and Syria," which set the stage for persistent Syrian intervention in Lebanon's internal affairs and infringement on its sovereignty. Predicated on "a common conception of the perils" facing the two countries, it requires that all organized activity in the military, security, political, and media realms of one country aimed at harming the other must be prevented, and that any individual or group seeking refuge in that country must, if deemed subversive, be arrested and handed over to the other country upon request. Thus, as the stronger of the two states, Syria can in theory invoke this provision of the treaty at will to seize, extradite, and imprison anyone or any group in Lebanon it alleges (however tenuously) is a security threat.[20] In fact, Syria has done exactly this on a number of occasions since 1991, as confirmed by independent human rights organizations within and outside of Lebanon.[21]

---

[18] For a discussion of the treaty and subsequent agreements, see Habib Malik, "Lebanon in the 1990s: Stability Without Freedom?" *Global Affairs* 7, no. 1, pp. 92-95. For a discussion of the Taif agreement and the Treaty of Brotherhood, see Fida Nasrallah, "The Treaty of Brotherhood, Cooperation and Coordination: An Assessment," ed. Youssef M. Choueiri, *State and Society in Syria and Lebanon* (New York: St. Martin's Press, 1993), pp. 103-11.

[19] See *al-Nahar*, May 23, 25, and 27, 1991.

[20] For the Arabic text of the agreement, see *al-Nahar*, September 7, 1991. The agreement further melds the two countries' security establishments by providing for periodic joint field exercises and the exchange of intelligence data, personnel, officers, and equipment.

[21] See also the 1992, 1993, and 1994 annual reports by the Foundation for Human and Humanitarian Rights, and assorted Amnesty International alerts and U.S. Department of State *Country Reports on Human Rights Practices* submitted to the U.S. House Committee on Foreign Affairs and the Senate Committee on Foreign Relations during the same period.

Other agreements followed soon thereafter. In early October, restrictions on overland travel were removed and duties on goods crossing the already porous Syria-Lebanon border were lowered. This led to a steadily rising influx into Lebanon of cheap and usually inferior Syrian products (which saturated the Lebanese market and forced many indigenous farmers and merchants out of business), and cheap Syrian labor, which led to Lebanese unemployment and ominous demographic changes.[22] Next came the draft of a health agreement that eventually paved the way for Syrian physicians trained in East Europe (not up to Western standards) to practice in Lebanon.[23]

The avalanche of agreements imposed on Lebanon subsided briefly in 1992, only to resume with vigor the following year. In March 1993 Syria and Lebanon signed an agreement to modernize telephone and other links and develop their telecommunications sectors. In May they finalized a tourism agreement creating a coordinated policy involving package tours and other joint approaches. Completing the work done two years earlier, an agreement was announced in June regulating land, sea, and air transportation between the two countries.[24] To coincide with the Israel-PLO Declaration of Principles (DoP) and the historic White House signing ceremony, in mid-September the Syrians unveiled four new agreements with Lebanon on agriculture and veterinary medicine, healthcare and pharmaceuticals, a socio-economic agreement aiming to create a common market for the two countries, and an agreement that further facilitated the movement of Syrian workers into Lebanon and their access to work permits under very favorable conditions once there.[25]

Syria's interest in solidifying its control over Lebanon focused on four areas: dismantling remaining border barriers and facilitating further transit of Syrians to and from Lebanon, strengthening educational and cultural integration, regulating the appropriation of portions of Lebanon's

---

[22] For the text of the border agreement, see *al-Hayat*, October 8, 1991. An earlier article spoke of the widespread presence of Syrian goods in Lebanese markets; see *al-Hayat*, July 15, 1991. Another mentioned "industrial integration" as a joint Syrian-Lebanese goal; see *al-Nahar*, September 11, 1991.

[23] *Al-Diyar*, December 10, 1991.

[24] For the Arabic text of the telecommunications agreement, see *al-Diyar*, March 22, 1993; for the tourism agreement, see *al-Nahar*, May 8, 1993; for the transportation agreement, see ibid., June 22, 1993.

[25] For the Arabic texts of the four agreements, along with extended commentary and official statements, see *al-Nahar*, September 17, 1993. As if to appease the dissenting voices alarmed by this string of bilateral agreements with Syria, the Lebanese government publicized a cultural, scientific, and technical agreement with France in October. The text of the agreement was fairly general, with emphasis on the importance of the French language, historical and cultural affinities with France, and the need for enhanced scientific and technical relations. Although a significant reaffirmation of close Lebanese-French ties, the agreement constituted a feeble antidote to the accelerated process of Syrianization unleashed by imposed bilateral agreements; for the Arabic text of the agreement between Lebanon and France, see *al-Diyar*, October 15, 1993.

water resources, and completing the integration of the two countries' agricultural sectors. In December 1993 a Lebanese-Syrian committee was set up to streamline and unify border tariffs and customs duties.[26] At a meeting in March 1994, the Lebanese-Syrian Security Committee (created by the Defense and Security Agreement) discussed ways to simplify bureaucratic procedures at border entry points and residency requirements for Syrians wishing to live and work in Lebanon. By June, the committee had drawn up specific recommendations on these issues for consideration by the Higher Council.[27] Meanwhile, the respective Lebanese and Syrian ministers of tourism signed a special document on increased tourism cooperation.[28]

In addition to signing three detailed follow-up protocols to the September 1993 agreement on agricultural and veterinary cooperation in the Bekaa city of Chtaura, a joint Lebanese-Syrian committee on electrical power took significant steps toward integrating the two countries' electricity systems by presenting a number of proposals including the construction of a joint power plant to be located just inside the Lebanese border.[29] Similarly, Syrian interest in Lebanese water resources dates back at least to the July 1991 meeting in Chtaura to discuss joint exploitation of the Orontes River—which originates in Lebanon and flows into Syria—and the Nahr Al-Kabir, which delineates Lebanon's northern border with Syria. Three years later, an agreement was concluded to erect a dam on the Orontes inside Lebanon and allot Lebanon 80 million cubic meters of the water to irrigate 6,000 hectares of fallow land in the Hirmel region.[30]

One of the most disturbing aspects of this artificial and enforced rapprochement is the Lebanese-Syrian cultural agreement. Apart from references to scientific and technical cooperation that appear alongside romanticized appeals to a presumed common folkloric heritage, the agreement contains specific provisions whose sole purpose is to accelerate Syria's absorption of Lebanon by obliterating the country's cultural distinctiveness. For example, the Syrians want a voice in the Lebanese government's policy plans for higher education, and the agreement speaks of forging closer ties between the government-run Lebanese University and Syrian universities, as well as similar Syrian links to Lebanon's private—and usually superior—universities. These steps would appear harmless were it not for accompanying calls to facilitate access for Syrian students to Lebanese institutions of higher learning and to officially recognize Syrian university degrees in Lebanon. The agreement also

---

[26] See *al-Nahar*, December 7, 1993.
[27] See ibid., March 21, June 24, 1994.
[28] See ibid., June 15, 1994.
[29] On the agricultural and veterinary protocols, see ibid., April 8, 1994; on the joint electrical power plant, see ibid., April 11, 1994.
[30] See ibid., July 29, 1991; September 21, 1994. For the Arabic text of the agreement on the waters of the Orontes River, see ibid., September 22, 1994.

encourages joint productions of films, plays, and other endeavors in the performing arts "with a view to serving the common cultural, civilizational, and national aspirations" of the two states.[31]

On the heels of the cultural agreement, Lebanon and Syria signed a postal protocol with three arresting points: the Syrian postal administration was put in charge of distributing the mail between the two countries; new Lebanese postage stamps would be printed in Syrian government printing facilities; and employees of the Lebanese postal service would attend regular training sessions in Syria at the special school run by the Syrian postal administration.[32]

A pattern appears to have been established whereby a spurt of bilateral agreements designed to legislate Lebanese subservience is timed to coincide with turns in the peace negotiations and other regional developments not necessarily to Syria's liking. In January 1996, for example, a series of agreements whose details remained shrouded in secrecy were revealed during delicate negotiations between Syria and Israel at the Wye Plantation in Maryland which apparently included the issue of future water rights on the Golan Heights. (They also coincided with renewed Syrian complaints about the dwindling downstream flow of the Euphrates River, due to the building of the Ataturk dam in Turkey.) Not surprisingly, the secret Syria-Lebanon agreements focused on solidifying economic ties (particularly in the areas of mutual investments and eliminating double taxation), establishing more joint processing centers at border crossings, and the sharing of water resources including for the first time specific references to the Litani River.[33]

Finally, to add insult to injury, the Syrian and Lebanese ministers of justice signed a September 1996 addendum to the 1951 Syrian-Lebanese judiciary agreement that tightened Damascus' official links with Lebanon's legal system by devising new mechanisms for extradition of criminals, exchange of information and legal publications, exchanging visits by judges and lawyers, and mutual recognition and application of the two countries' civil and commercial laws.[34]

Though much of what is in these treaties and agreements is seemingly innocuous, their sheer volume and the speed with which they were devised

---

[31] For the Arabic text of the Syrian-Lebanese cultural agreement, see *al-Safir*, May 12, and *al-Nahar*, September 22, 1994.

[32] For the details, see *al-Hayat*, August 18, 1995.

[33] See *al-Nahar*, January 29, 1996. In a daring front-page editorial in the same issue, editor-in-chief and leading Lebanese journalist Ghassan Tueini openly rejected the moves toward "unification" with Syria, citing as one reason the enormous disparities in the two countries' political and economic systems. Such dreams of unification, Tueini wrote, "will be dashed on the shoals of freedom and reality." He noted the many areas in which Lebanese society had excelled because of its high level of freedom, and concluded by calling for cooperation with Syria on the basis of the principle of reciprocity. His defiant rejection of outright unity was itself a major news story.

[34] See *al-Hayat*, September 25 and 27, 1996.

and legislated—coupled with the complete absence of Lebanese sovereignty as the process was unfolding—offers tangible cause for concern. Although news accounts occasionally suggest that the Syrian economy, and Syrian society in general, are gradually opening up and that the Lebanese-Syrian agreements ought to be understood in this context, little comfort should be derived from such misplaced optimism.[35] With a new, pro-Syria parliament in Lebanon, more binding agreements can be expected, the cumulative effect of which will be to further erode Lebanon's special distinguishing features and contributions and increasingly mold it into a dull appendage of its larger neighbor.

THE DEMOGRAPHIC DRAGON

Accurate demographic statistics have never been an abundant commodity in Lebanon. The first and last official population census was conducted in 1932. It indicated a clear Christian majority. No scientific second attempt has since been made; the entire subject remains controversial.[36] Since then and particularly after the outbreak of the

---

[35] In one article, an unnamed Lebanese government official spoke about the "new orientation in the Syrian economy toward the free market, with privatization in some sectors and free transactions in others, all of which brings the two economies of Lebanon and Syria closer to one another along the lines of cooperation witnessed in the European Common Market"; see *al-Nahar*, September 21, 1994. The alleged "new orientation" is in fact still largely a mirage, and whatever "free transactions" are occurring and profits being reaped are conducted by a few in the ruling class. Syria's much-hailed Investment Law No. 10 of 1991 has made only embryonic moves toward a free-enterprise economy. There is a long way to go, and only a fully sovereign Lebanon can make a difference. Moreover, given the profound dissimilarities in the two economies of Lebanon and Syria, any comparisons with the homogeneous European Union are ridiculous.

[36] Feigning scientific accuracy, a demographic study commissioned by the Hariri Foundation in 1991 relied for its population estimates on data purportedly collected during a food distribution drive funded by the Saudis and conducted by foundation volunteers throughout Lebanon. It claims to reveal that the Christians are 35 percent of the total population of Lebanon, but the methodology is highly questionable due to the many irregularities and extrapolations involved, and the results are even less reliable. The study ends with what amounts to crass warnings directed at the Christians and is meant to dissuade them from harboring future political aspirations. It is indicative of the vitriol surrounding the issue of demography; see Muhammad Faour, "The Demography of Lebanon: a Reappraisal," *Middle Eastern Studies* 27, no. 4 (October 1991), pp. 631-41.

A quasi-official attempt at a door-to-door census was carried out over a two-year period beginning in 1994. It yielded the following figures published by the government in October 1996: Lebanon's overall population stands at 3.1 million (less than previously estimated); 150,000 deaths (probably inflated) as a direct result of the 1975-90 war; several hundred thousand Lebanese left the country because of the war (this is accurate); Mount Lebanon contains 36.8 percent of the total population, the highest demographic concentration; those below age fifteen make up 29.2 percent of the population; those between ages fifteen and sixty-four constitute 63.8 percent; those over sixty-five are 6.9 percent; and 33.6 percent of those who left Lebanon since 1993 hold university degrees. No statistical data on

Lebanon war in 1975, two broad trends can be discerned: a steady decline in the Christian birth rate as compared with the rising Muslim rate, and an increase in Christian emigration dramatically hastened in the past twenty years by the events of the war. Despite these trends, however, the various Christians in Lebanon remain a sizable minority—some estimates range as high as 40-45 percent of the population, with the Maronites being the largest sub-group.[37] The Shi'a constitute by far the largest community among the Muslims.

Were these trends allowed to follow a more or less natural course, Lebanon's multi-religious society would remain delicately balanced for the foreseeable future with no overwhelmingly uncontested majorities. This would of necessity require that any viable political formula for coexistence continue to rest on the principle of communal consensus. In recent years, however, some alarming developments have intruded—often by design— upon Lebanon and drastically upset the demographic balance in what has become the region's most densely populated country. These include the Lebanon war, the influx of Syrian workers, the 1994 Naturalization Decree, and the resultant naturalization of Palestinian refugees.

The Impact of the War

Years of war in Lebanon have resulted in an undetermined number of civilian fatalities on all sides. Although accurate figures are difficult to obtain, it is reasonable to assume that the various communities were culled more or less proportionally. The war also caused massive internal population displacement, with a tendency toward segregation along confessional lines. The predominantly Christian eastern parts of Beirut became even more so throughout the war years, and a similar process occurred in the majority Muslim western sections of the city. Mixed West Beirut neighborhoods such as Ras Beirut and Musaitbeh experienced a brisk Christian exodus. In the Shuf mountains east and south of Beirut, sectarian clashes between Christians and Druze led to massacres and an "ethnic cleansing" of the region's Christians, who fled in huge numbers to already congested Christian parts of Mount Lebanon to the north.[38] Since

---

confessional breakdowns was given; see *al-Hayat*, October 15, and *Washington Times*, October 16, 1996.

[37] The demographic picture is further complicated by the ongoing dispute over Lebanese expatriates who, despite living abroad—often as citizens of other countries—continue to hold valid Lebanese passports, own property or thriving businesses in Lebanon, visit the country frequently, have family residing there, and clamor for voting rights. The vast majority of these expatriates are Christian. In the 1992 parliamentary elections, Minister of the Interior Sami Al-Khatib relied on voter registration lists indicating that 48 percent of those eligible and registered to vote were Christians and 52 percent were Muslims.

[38] According to one Western scholar, eight out of ten massacre victims during the war years were Christian, and the targeting of Christians was in most cases deliberate, with the aim of terrorizing the community and inducing mass population dislocations; see Theodor Hanf, *Coexistence in Wartime Lebanon: Decline of a State and Rise of a Nation* (London: Centre for Lebanese Studies in association with I. B. Tauris, 1993), p. 342.

the cessation of hostilities in 1989-90, some dislocated Christians have been slowly returning to previously mixed areas in Beirut, but a return to the Druze-dominated Shuf mountains is still hampered by lingering psychological fears.

For their part, wealthy Sunni Muslim families are increasingly purchasing apartments and real estate in the Christian areas of the mountains overlooking Beirut. Some spend only the summer months there, but others intend to take up permanent residence in their new homes among the Christians. An increasing number of affluent Muslims are also acquiring ski chalets at the higher elevations of Mount Lebanon. Moreover, there is a gradual Shi'a demographic surge from the south and the adjoining coastal region toward the Shuf and the crowded southern suburbs of Beirut, which is causing concern among Druze and Sunnis alike.

Emigration, particularly of Christians, increased during the war years. Among the preferred destinations were France, Canada, and the United States, with Australia, Latin America, Cyprus, and Great Britain not far behind. The numbers of Lebanese working in West Africa (mostly Christians and Shi'a) and the Persian Gulf (mixed, but mainly Christians and Sunnis) at first swelled and then began to decline somewhat. Since the early 1990s, many Lebanese (particularly Shi'a) have returned from some of the West African states that were experiencing either political turmoil, outbursts of xenophobic hostility, or both. On the whole this group has tended to bring back to the country substantial amounts of capital, much of which has been invested in building or reconstruction and renovation. Again, exact figures are elusive, but the community that seems to have suffered the most depletion in its numbers in recent years due to emigration has been the Christians.

Syrian Workers

Perhaps the Lebanon war's most worrying demographic legacy is the massive influx of outsiders—overwhelmingly Syrians. The first official indication of this came in early October 1991 with the announcement of the preliminary agreement to remove travel barriers between Syria and Lebanon, especially at the overland border crossings.[39] Between 1991 and 1994, successive agreements and arrangements were put into effect ostensibly to regulate the flow of people and goods across the frontiers, but in fact to make it easier and virtually undetectable for large numbers of Syrians to enter Lebanon. This culminated in the October 1994 "Lebanese-Syrian Bilateral Agreement on Labor."[40] Among other things, the agreement required equal treatment of workers in the other country; joint border processing centers for seasonal workers requiring temporary permits; a special agency in each country's Ministry of Labor to deal with

---

[39] See footnote 22.

[40] For the Arabic text of the labor agreement, see *al-Nahar*, October 19, 1994.

the other's workers; a passing reference to Lebanon's offering Syrian workers social security, health, and work-related insurance; and a provision that the agreement be made retroactive to workers already employed prior to the agreement. Though these items may not sound all that bad, given the preponderance of Syria's influence in Lebanon, the implementation of these provisions will more than likely come at the latter's expense.

Writing on the shadowy world of Lebanese statistics in the Beirut daily *al-Nahar* a few days before the proclamation of the labor agreement, Michel Murkos noted the loopholes in the agreement and offered some immigration estimates. Until the agreement, he said, it had been standard procedure not to issue entry permits to Syrian and Palestinian workers coming from Syria. Lebanese employers preferred these low-wage workers, however, and usually employed them "under the table" (i.e., illegally). Thus, no entry or employment records exist for them and they remain unaccounted for in surveys or statistical compilations. The official Lebanese Ministry of Labor figure for registered Syrian workers with valid work contracts in 1993, for example, is a mere 34,872.

To obtain a more accurate picture of the overall influx of foreigners—specifically Syrians—into Lebanon, Murkos resorted to Lebanese Bureau of General Security records on the number of people entering and leaving the country. In 1993, these records indicate that 1,108,587 Syrians entered Lebanon and 660,681 left—implying that at the end of the year 447,906 Syrians remained in the country. Figures for the first half of 1994 similarly reveal 937,158 Syrians entering and 534,408 leaving, implying that 402,749 stayed in Lebanon.[41] Murkos revisited the subject months later in a renewed attempt to ascertain the numbers, again using entry and departure figures compiled by the Bureau of General Security. From 1993 to June 1995, there was a net gain of 1,435,991 Syrians in Lebanon.[42] These new residents were not all tourists and non-working visitors; obviously, clandestine hiring of great numbers of Syrians—mainly in agriculture, construction, and the service sector—was a widespread practice.

Bearing in mind the limitations of these figures due to undocumented Syrian migration, they nevertheless offer a reasonable indication of the astounding gravity of the situation. Lebanon's population is conservatively estimated at about 3.5 million. (This takes into account the roughly 50,000 casualties and 900,000 Lebanese who left the country during the war years, and another 150,000 who exited in between 1993 and mid-1995.) In addition, there are nearly 1.2 million Syrians residing in Lebanon—in other words, for every two Lebanese in Lebanon, there is one Syrian living there as well! More importantly, the overwhelming majority of the latter are able-bodied young men between the ages of eighteen and forty-five, which means they probably *outnumber* the Lebanese in the same demographic group. Moreover, these estimates are based on "known"

---

[41] *Al-Nahar*, October 14, 1994.
[42] Ibid., July 24, 1995.

figures and do not include Syrian soldiers (who supposedly number around 40,000), the unseen intelligence presence, or civilians fleeing harsh economic conditions in Syria who enter Lebanon surreptitiously to seek undeclared employment.

The trend evidenced by the entry and exit figures since 1993 is an alarming rise in Lebanese emigration aggravated by a relentless increase in Syrian arrivals—a veritable population transfer. If this trend continues, it will mean among other things that the Lebanese labor force will be predominantly Syrian in the not-too-distant future. There are already an estimated 30,000 Syrian vegetable vendors with mobile carts roaming the streets of Beirut and its suburbs and doubling as an intelligence and security apparatus. Because foreign workers are not taxed under Lebanese law, this results in growing losses of revenue not only for the private sector but also for the government. Hard currency is being siphoned out of Lebanon at a rate that drastically affects the country's balance of payments.

The awesome economic consequences of these developments pale into insignificance, however, when compared to the catastrophic effect on Lebanon's fragile demographic balance—which is nothing short of a movement toward Syrian colonization of Lebanon. As hundreds of thousands of Syrians move into Lebanon, they could potentially decide to settle in the country, perhaps marrying locally or eventually bringing their existing families in Syria over to join them. Many are seeking ways of obtaining Lebanese citizenship and finding the authorities more than willing to oblige. Moreover, almost all of the incoming Syrians are Muslim. In an interview in the London-based weekly magazine *al-Wasat*, Syrian Vice President Abdelhalim Khaddam was asked to comment on growing Lebanese fears about the massive influx of Syrian workers. It is not Syria that sends these workers to Lebanon, he replied, but rather the Lebanese who open the way. Lebanon, he noted with some degree of truth, was built by Syrian manpower.[43] What he did not address was the obvious linkage between the phenomenally steep rise in the number of Syrians entering and staying in Lebanon in recent years, and Syria's overwhelmingly dominant political and military posture in Lebanon. The Syrian workers who came to Lebanon in the past (i.e., prior to *pax Syriana*) were strictly monitored and controlled; once their jobs were finished and their work permits expired, they had to leave. That control by the Lebanese authorities has all but disappeared.

The Naturalization Decree

Perhaps the single most damaging event in the sordid tale of demographic manipulation in post-Taif Lebanon has been Naturalization Decree No. 5247, proclaimed on June 20, 1994. With one stroke, the Beirut government decided to grant Lebanese citizenship to roughly 300,000 individuals—more than 70 percent of whom (some estimates say

---

[43] *Al-Wasat*, November 20, 1995.

as much as 85 percent) were Syrians.[44] Though it normally makes sense to treat the many conspiracy theories rampant in the Middle East with an attitude of healthy skepticism, an exception should be made in the case of the 1994 Naturalization Decree: It is the closest thing to a carefully crafted conspiracy designed to alter Lebanon's demography one can imagine, and it has Syrian fingerprints all over it.

Many of the people affected by this decree had their cases pending before the Lebanese authorities for years. Some were resident Palestinians or Kurds, others came from other Arab states, and some were stateless Arab nomads of the Wadi Khaled tribe who inhabit mostly the region of north-east Lebanon, and regularly move back and forth across the Lebanon-Syria border. The bulk of the remainder, however—which is to say, the majority—were Syrians, mostly newly-arrived workers. For the Lebanese government to proceed with this naturalization *en masse* without taking the time to probe each case carefully to make sure criminal and other undesirable elements are weeded out in advance, represents the height of irresponsibility and recklessness.

In addition, this sinister process of naturalization involved several flagrant irregularities. The ratio of Christians to Muslims among the naturalized group is roughly three to seven. In many instances, however, scores of naturalized people and families were counted as Christians when in fact they were not. A number of Alawis—the ruling minority sect in Syria—were naturalized and then "registered" as Maronites. Some of the naturalized Wadi Khaled nomad Arabs were in actuality Syrian intelligence officers. Polygamy and cases of fake marriages swelled the numbers of naturalized Muslims—in one case, a father was registered as "married" to his daughter so that her children (now registered as her brothers and sisters) from a Kurdish man could be naturalized as Lebanese.

Once naturalized, the new citizens have to be registered in a particular district for electoral and other administrative purposes. There was a distinct trend toward registering large numbers of Muslims in Christian areas in order to dilute the demographic composition. Minister of Interior Michel Murr, for example, a Greek Orthodox Christian and member of parliament, saw to it that individuals and families were registered in his electoral district in Mount Lebanon with the understanding that they would vote for him to retain his parliamentary seat. In August 1996, they faithfully did just that.

The practice of wholesale naturalization—offering Lebanese citizenship indiscriminately to tens of thousands of people—has the potential to create other unwelcome complications. Nothing prevents many of these newly naturalized citizens, who lack roots in the country and thus an attachment to the land, from leaving Lebanon at the first opportunity, armed with a valid passport and a new "identity." This has

---

[44] Most of the statistics and other information in this section were obtained from an anonymous source in the Central Census Department of the Lebanese Ministry of Interior.

frequently been the case in the past with naturalized Egyptians, Armenians, Syrians, Palestinians, and others. Many naturalized Christian Arabs fall into this category and use Lebanon only as a "stepping stone" to emigrate out of the region altogether. While Christians leave, however, their naturalized Muslim counterparts remain, thereby further disrupting Lebanon's delicate and already strained demographic balance.

Palestinian Naturalization

There has been much speculation about the fate of the roughly 400,000[45] Palestinians living in Lebanon: Will all or some be "repatriated" to a future Palestinian entity as part of a comprehensive Middle East peace deal? Will they be "redistributed" in varying proportions among Arab countries? Will they remain in Lebanon and be issued Palestinian passports or special "interim status" papers pending a final resolution of their situation? Or will they be naturalized as Lebanese and thrown into the boiling demographic cauldron that Lebanon threatens to become?

The vast majority of these Palestinians are Sunni Muslim. Many trace their (or their parents') arrival in Lebanon to 1948; others ended up in Lebanon after the 1970 exodus from Jordan or were "dumped" in the country during the 1975-76 Lebanon war.[46] They tend to be concentrated in deteriorating refugee camps in and around the coastal cities of Sidon, Tyre, and Tripoli. They have to contend with latent ill feelings toward them from many quarters inside Lebanon, particularly the Christians and Shi'a. And many of these Palestinians recognize the precariousness of their situation and the uncertain future that awaits them.

Lebanon cannot absorb such a vast number of Sunni Palestinians and remain stable. Yet many are already being naturalized surreptitiously using forged papers and phony identities under the cover of the 1994 Naturalization Decree. The only conceivable way some of these Palestinians can be accepted as Lebanese without creating an uproar is if the affected communities (mainly the Shi'a and Christians) can be compensated politically through constitutionally grounded guarantees that preserve individual and communal rights for all regardless of demographic fluctuations; in other words, by legislating safeguards that protect Lebanon's pluralist character and consensus political arrangements.

To outsiders, Lebanon's labyrinthine demographics may seem a hopeless abyss, but the situation is not as desperate as it appears. The problem hinges largely on the unlikely indefinite perpetuation of Lebanon's current political captivity under Syria; even a slight restoration of Lebanese sovereignty—the beginnings of an inevitable thaw of the Syrian ice—would quickly transform a seemingly intractable situation into

---

[45] According to a well-researched and documented article on the increase in the number of Palestinians residing in Lebanon during 1948-95, by 1995 the total was between 400,000 and 450,000; see *al-Nahar*, December 1, 1995.

[46] Most of the latter were guerillas and their families who had been living in Syria and Iraq.

a more manageable one. As confidence in Lebanon was slowly restored, large numbers of Lebanese who left the country during the past twenty years of turmoil would return; some have already returned since the cessation of hostilities in 1990. Most of these returnees would be Christians and their arrival would restore some of the much-needed balance to Lebanon's demography.

A more sovereign government in Beirut could also reinstate tighter controls on the influx of foreigners into Lebanon and their activities once there. Outright nullification of the 1994 Naturalization Decree would violate the basic human rights of many people, but the government could take several steps to ease its deleterious impact: set up a special registry of newly naturalized citizens, whose names would be kept for a specified period of time pending a thorough review of their naturalizations; readjust the districts in which the newly naturalized were registered to ensure they do not excessively distort confessional homogeneity; and prohibit these newly naturalized citizens from voting or running for public office for at least eight years after becoming Lebanese.

An enhancement of Lebanese sovereignty would also allow a more serious examination of the issue of granting voting rights to non-residents who continue to hold Lebanese citizenship—a step that would help redress some of the demographic asymmetries. With the improvement of the overall political climate, consensus politics could once again be practiced among the various Lebanese communities and the natural rate of demographic increase within each community could be accommodated by unequivocal constitutional safeguards for basic individual and communal rights.

III

The Economics of Autocracy

Any attempt to make sense of the murky microcosm that is Lebanon's post-war economy must by necessity start (and most likely also end) with the controversial central figure in the whole faulty edifice: Rafiq Hariri. His peculiar approach to his dual role as prime minister and pivotal figure in the ailing Lebanese economy has been aptly described as the "politics of tycoonism."[1] This raises the immediate question of why a multi-billionaire like Hariri would want to be prime minister of Lebanon and would spare no effort in 1996 to get elected to parliament. Many in Lebanon believe that Hariri sought these positions because he believed that Lebanon could be turned into another of his many lucrative business propositions. With his solid Saudi credentials—as a personal protégé of King Fahd—and financial empire, Hariri became prime minister in 1992 with the overt task of initiating Lebanon's post-war reconstruction. Along with this lofty aim, however, critics soon discerned a specific political mandate and an Islamicizing agenda which, coupled with Hariri's dismal economic performance, constitute the source of the lingering controversy that surrounds him.

To be fair, Hariri's program has yielded some "positive" achievements for the Lebanese economy. Since becoming prime minister in 1992, he has managed to stabilize the faltering Lebanese currency at the steady level of around 1,500 Lebanese lira to the U.S. dollar. Though necessary, this has proved to be a double-edged sword in that, like everything else in the economy, the lira's fortunes have become tied to those of Hariri himself. On the three occasions he threatened to resign due to bickering with certain Syrian-chosen ministers in his cabinet, the lira teetered on the brink and actually began to collapse.

This in turn reveals another of his achievements: a symbiotic working relationship with the chief powerbrokers in Lebanon, the Syrians. This cozy and mutually beneficial relationship—whereby senior Syrian officials and their sons receive "offers" and "opportunities" via Hariri for lucrative contracts in Saudi Arabia and elsewhere in return for Hariri's keeping his job and relative freedom in the areas that matter most to him—has undeniably provided a degree of artificial continuity and stability to post-

---

[1] The author first heard the term from Fouad Ajami of the School of Advanced International Studies at Johns Hopkins University, who said he heard it from Jamil Mroueh, chief editor of the Beirut *Daily Star*.

Taif Lebanon. For the sake of their own prestige and the profits they are reaping in Lebanon, the Syrians would not allow Hariri to resign, and they moved quickly to silence or distance his abrasive critics in the government. Having Hariri at the helm has also inspired some confidence in certain wealthy Arab investors, who have diverted meager amounts of their vast fortunes to Lebanese banks and made modest pledges of investment in Hariri's reconstruction projects, all as a means of testing the waters of the supposedly reviving Lebanese economy.

Hariri also enjoyed a very cozy relationship with French President Jacques Chirac, who visited Lebanon in April 1996 and was warmly received by Hariri on both occasions. Several other 1996 events boosted Hariri's political standing locally and enhanced his stature as an international statesman. In the wake of Israel's April "Operation Grapes of Wrath," Hariri made his presence felt in the regional political arena as a hands-on negotiator and "voice of moderation," winning him significant points in Washington and other important capitals. His impressive showing at the polls in Lebanon's Syrian-choreographed parliamentary elections that summer produced the country's largest parliamentary bloc, under his direct control. In addition, Hariri's October brief visit with President Clinton at the White House, and a December "Friends of Lebanon" economic conference he convened in Washington also constitute impressive achievements and served to alert the Syrians to his swiftly growing prominence on the international scene. On every occasion, it was apparent that Hariri's capitalist consumerism and big business style could not co-exist for long with the "death wish" culture and martyr mentality peddled by Hezbollah. Clashes (at least of interest) were inevitable and did occur in both cases.

THE RECONSTRUCTION QUANDARY

Behind the hype and glitter surrounding Hariri's reconstruction program, however, lay the sordid reality of his economic shortsightedness, apparent disregard for the welfare of ordinary people, and unabashed self-promotion. The grand reconstruction schemes focus almost exclusively on downtown Beirut's destroyed commercial center, leaving the outlying parts of the city and the rest of the country virtually untouched. Hariri's concept of rebuilding the downtown caters exclusively to the country's pre-war strengths in trade, finance, and service sectors, while neglecting totally the economy's other vital components, namely industry and agriculture.[2]

Moreover, his approach in many ways represents the antithesis of *laissez faire* economics, resembling instead a primitive example of centralized

---

[2] Little has been done, for example, about the city's horrendous traffic congestion and shortage of parking spaces beyond proposing a multi-million dollar "ring" highway that disregards clogged intersections and the enormous pollution problem.

statism—flagrant monopolistic capitalism (to borrow a Marxist term)—run amuck.[3] Showcase projects such as the new sports stadium (inaugurated in July 1997), convention center, enlargement of Beirut airport, and upgrading of the Beirut-Damascus highway received all of the scarce funds (and publicity), while badly needed improvements in the crumbling infrastructure (e.g., electricity, telephones, sewage, drainage, and roads) of the capital and other towns and villages were pushed further down on the list of government priorities. Serious attention to these essentials did not commence until the spring of 1995, more than two years after Hariri took office, and the work done thus far has been sloppy and uncoordinated.

Hariri created a real estate company called Solidere that has undertaken the reconstruction of downtown Beirut, and has been the subject of acrimonious debate since its inception. From a number of perspectives—legal, architectural, sociological, financial, and economic—Solidere's defects appear legion.[4] To begin with, the company expropriated property in and around the city center at far less than market value, and "compensated" their owners with shares in the company itself. This resulted in an immediate outcry, led by a group of mostly Sunni property owners and merchants from established Beirut families such as the Daouks. Hariri's honeymoon with his Sunni supporters came to a speedy end, and the bandwagon of hostile criticism against his policies was soon joined by a number of lackluster Sunni political leaders frustrated at being overshadowed by the determined tycoon.

The Shi'a were also dissatisfied because they felt Hariri's focus on the downtown area ignored Beirut's impoverished southern suburbs teeming with dislocated Shi'a families from South Lebanon. The uproar reached its climax when Hezbollah spiritual leader Sheikh Muhammad Hussein

---

[3] Many articles have criticized various aspects of Hariri's reconstruction plans and programs. One of the better examples, by Hazim Saghieh, discusses both the flaws in the approaches to reconstruction and their collateral political fallout; see *al-Hayat*, September 28, 1996. Saghieh at one point criticizes the marginalization of the role of the Christians in the entire reconstruction process; it is thanks to such minority communities, he asserts, that freedom and a vibrant parliamentary life, both of which are necessary prerequisites for any sustained capitalist growth, have historically flourished.

[4] Criticism of Solidere has been mounting since the early 1990s. The opening shot came in a study by a group of constitutional-legal, economic, social, and technical experts relating to post-war reconstruction; see Nabil Bayhum, et al., *I'mar Bayrut wal Fursa Da'i'ah: Wasat Bayrut Al-tijari wa-Sharika Al-'iqariyya—Al-waqa'ih, Al-murtakazat, Al-bada'il (Reconstruction of Beirut and the Lost Opportunity: Beirut's Commercial Center and the Real Estate Company—The Facts, the Assumptions, the Alternatives)* (Beirut: Rami Al-Khal Printing House, 1992). Each of the authors went on to publish articles and, in some cases, books on the subject. With the help of grants from the Ford Foundation and other local foundations, four critical books appeared in 1995, the most prominent among them was Nabil Bayhum, *Al-i'mar wal Maslaha Al-'amma fi Al-ijtima' wa Thaqafa: M'ana Al-Madina Sukkanuha (Reconstruction and the Public Interest in the Social and Cultural Domains: The City Acquires Meaning through Its Inhabitants)* (Beirut: Dar Al-Jadid in cooperation with the Foundation for Urban Research and the Ford Foundation, 1995). For a review, see *al-Hayat*, December 17, 1995. This section on Solidere relies mainly on these two books.

Fadlallah issued a religious ruling (*fatwa*) prohibiting the purchase of shares in Solidere.⁵ Hariri moved quickly to assuage Shi'a protests by proposing a scheme called "Elissar" to develop the city's southern suburbs. It consists of a comprehensive housing plan designed to give the sprawling Shi'a shantytowns around the Beirut airport an urban face-lift. The project has also served as an occasion for Hariri to open channels with Hezbollah through joint business dealings.⁶

As a result of the policy of compensating property owners with Solidere stock—and a rush to acquire shares by wealthy Arabs and Lebanese at home and abroad—the net value of Solidere subscriptions initially rose to approximately $650 million. Although company regulations ostensibly provide "safeguards" against overwhelming foreign ownership of shares and property in the commercial city center, the efficacy of these paper guarantees is offset by the widespread practice of buying and selling land and company assets to practically anyone, Lebanese or foreign, through the use of third parties and "front companies" designed to conceal the true identity of the purchaser.⁷ In fact this practice is commonly attributed to Hariri's personal business dealings, and illustrates the confusion and damage that can result when the interests of the public domain are allowed to overlap with those of the private individual.

The disproportionate foreign element in Lebanon's economic revival will undoubtedly have ominous political repercussions as well. With the emergence of Hariri and his hand-picked associates (sprinkled with an untold number of foreign magnates) as the new post-war plutocracy in Lebanon, small and medium-sized Lebanese businessmen, merchants, and shopkeepers are being squeezed right out of the much-heralded economic recovery. Beirut's *centre ville* is in danger of losing its distinctive cachet as it is systematically emptied of its once-thriving entrepreneurial middle class, the backbone of any healthy economy, in favor of the mega-rich with foreign strings attached. This lament is not merely a nostalgic stroll down the memory lane of a bygone Beirut; it points to an alarming feature of Solidere's plans for reconstruction transcending economics and even politics: an all-out assault on culture.

ARCHAEOLOGICAL "CLEANSING"

Nothing better exposes Solidere's war on culture than the deplorable fate of archaeology in downtown Beirut. According to the Hariri vision of reconstruction, the city of Beirut is little more than a pile of rubble in search of dollars to stack it up neatly and properly again. From the outset,

---

⁵ See *al-Safir*, January 10, 1994.
⁶ The "Elissar" project was created in April 1995 through governmental Decree No. 6918. For more on Elissar, see *al-Nahar*, February 8, 1996; and *al-Safir*, February 9, 1996.
⁷ See *I'mar Bayrut wal Fursa Da'i'ah*, p. 48.

Hariri made three erroneous assumptions: that the peace process between Israel and the Arabs would move quickly toward a final conclusion, that large amounts of foreign capital and investments would pour into Lebanon fairly swiftly as a result, and that little of archaeological significance would be uncovered in the downtown section of Beirut slated for reconstruction. In fact, the peace process has taken a long time and may have even stalled; the anticipated foreign investment never occurred; and a great deal of significant archaeology began to be unearthed in precisely those areas of Beirut that Solidere's mammoth bulldozers were busy digging.

Incapable of appreciating the significance of archaeology (or worse, deliberately wanting to obliterate Beirut's uniquely rich multi-cultural heritage) and unwilling to alter its preset blueprints and rigid design plans, Solidere stubbornly ignored all advice to the contrary and literally plowed ahead with its bulldozers, wrecking balls, and dynamite charges. Over and over again, a sad spectacle was brutally reenacted: a multi-layered site of successive civilizations would be uncovered—where diverse cultures from the Bronze Age through the Phoenician, Hellenic, and Roman centuries to the Byzantine, Arab, Crusader, and Ottoman periods had painstakingly preserved the glories erected by their predecessors while carefully depositing their own—only to be erased forever by the bulldozer's undiscriminating teeth. The Lebanon war had destroyed what was standing above ground, and Solidere annihilated what was slumbering beneath it.[8]

Specialists in Near Eastern and Mediterranean archaeology from all over the world began to flock to Beirut as word went out about the incredible treasures being excavated there. Among them was the world-famous French archaeologist Jean Lauffray, who spent most of his life studying ancient Lebanese civilizations, particularly in Byblos and Beirut. Feeling the rising heat of publicity generated by the excavations,[9] Solidere decided it needed to mount a public relations campaign to absorb the growing criticism of its callous disregard for archaeological ruins. It created a department to handle matters related to archaeology, in an

---

[8] In September 1995, the author attended a panel discussion and slide presentation on the archaeological digs in the center of the city, which was sponsored by the Foundation for Human and Humanitarian Rights Lebanon (FHHR/L), a member of the Paris-based Federation Internationale des Droits de l'Homme. The panel featured May Abboud Abi-Akl, *al-Nahar*'s renowned reporter for cultural affairs, and Ibrahim Kuwatli, Lebanese University professor of archaeology, who is also the UNESCO coordinator for the Beirut archaeological sites. Professor Kuwatli's moving slide presentation showed examples of uncovered sites replete with a rich assortment of archaeological finds *before* Solidere's bulldozers got to them, and the same sites *after* the bulldozers had done their grim work of consigning history to oblivion. The experience was, to put it mildly, nauseating.

[9] Beirut's leading daily *al-Nahar* pursued a relentless campaign of highlighting the issue of archaeology in its pages starting in early 1994. Other papers and local media outlets soon followed *al-Nahar*'s lead, thus sensitizing public opinion and creating pressure on government and Solidere officials. Eventually the issue reached the BBC and CNN, where it had limited but effective exposure in a few of their broadcasts.

attempt to convey the impression that the company was sensitive to the impact of reconstruction on culture, but actually did little to modify its original masterplan to accommodate emerging archaeological finds. Emboldened by its own gimmickry, Solidere then invited a group of experts, including Lauffray, to come to Beirut and survey the new digs.

Lauffray arrived in Beirut in October 1994 and after touring the sites, met with Hariri. His message was simple and straightforward: within a roughly one-square kilometer area in downtown Beirut, there were forty-two distinct archaeological sites, each revealing a magnificent superimposition of civilizations and ancient cultures unprecedented in any city. To the greatest degree possible, he said, they should be preserved and integrated into a reworked version of Hariri's reconstruction scheme that would then attract scholars from all over the world along with millions of tourists. In particular, Lauffray concentrated on an old Phoenician city and port that were uncovered during the clearing of derelict buildings gutted by the fighting along the sea front. Within a few months, 80 percent of this invaluable Phoenician discovery, including a unique network of furnaces used for making glass, was bulldozed out of existence. He was also interested in the site of the famous Roman School of Law and adjoining Roman Forum, both of which had been destroyed in an earthquake in 555 A.D. Lauffray knew that the location of the Roman complex extended beneath the present site of Lebanon's parliament building and a nearby bank.

In his discussions with Hariri, Shi'a Speaker of Parliament Berri, and Solidere officials, Lauffray emphasized the importance of the archaeological troves for the common cultural heritage of humanity, and referred to a 1978 UNESCO agreement declaring such ruins part of that collective heritage. The case was compellingly self-evident and needed little justification: In the era of the Byzantine emperor Justinian, Beirut had been the unrivaled seat of legislation and legal learning for the entire ancient world, and the laws formulated there became the foundations of the Western legal code. Lauffray received solemn assurances from Lebanese leaders that everything would be done to preserve the finds for display. When asked to offer practical suggestions, he presented several plans to either save the ruins while maintaining much of the existing structures above them, or excavate and move them to other locations. A committee was formed to study the proposals and implement the most suitable, and Lauffray returned to France.

When some months later his letters to Hariri and Solidere went unanswered, Lauffray learned to his great dismay that in April, Berri had violated their agreement and started to remove a part of the Roman Forum in order to install underground parking for parliamentary representatives and their employees. Solidere had once again revealed its true colors as a crass commercial enterprise driven by the lust for quick profits, and ready to sacrifice everything in its way for the sake of material gain. Lauffray published a scathing indictment of Solidere and its boss,

Hariri, and an appeal on behalf of humanity's common heritage for the preservation of Beirut's archaeological treasures.[10]

Though even a much less astute businessman could see that preserving these valuable archaeological sites would generate windfall tourism revenues, Hariri apparently had other, more pressing items on his politically charged agenda that took precedence over archaeology's potential commercial lure. Some of his staunchest critics among the Christians, for example, view him (perhaps exaggeratedly) as the spearhead of an insidious form of Islamicization backed by Saudi coffers and out to "create facts" on the ground, whether through extensive land purchases in predominantly Christian areas or through the deliberate destruction of Beirut's pre-Islamic archaeological relics for fear that the city's Christian past—or worse, some version of Phoenicianism as an ideology—may be resurrected.

Some of Hariri's actions seem to lend credence to these accusations. He insists, for example, that what he calls the "Arab highway"—the proposed widening and upgrading of part of the Beirut-Damascus highway to be financed by a toll system—pass through the middle of specific Christian towns and villages such as Kahhaleh and Hazmieh, requiring that much of the town be defaced or destroyed in the process. This has raised Christian suspicions about his real motives in targeting the areas that were on the dividing line during the Lebanon war and put up stiff resistance to anti-Christian forces attacking from the other side—that what was not accomplished by the gun is now being carried out by a more subtle (but equally effective) weapon: the Solidere bulldozer.[11] The fanfare that surrounded the June 1997 visits of Malaysian Prime Minister Mahathir bin Mohamad and Saudi Crown Prince Abdullah, along with the many bilateral agreements Lebanon concluded with the two influential Muslim states, heightened Christian suspicions that Hariri's international connections are tilted in a decidedly Islamic direction.

Christians are not alone in harboring apprehensions about Hariri. Some radical Shi'a feel that his Saudi-backed policies compete with the Iran-inspired version of Islamicization that they are working to spread in

---

[10] For Lauffray's views, see "Beyrouth: Ce qui n'a pas été dit," *Archeologia* 317 (November 1995), pp. 4-11. For background information, see also ibid., no. 316 (October 1995). For an extended analysis of Lauffray's Beirut visit and subsequent disappointment, see May Abboud Abi-Akl in *al-Nahar*, November 16, 1995. A group of the property owners whose land in downtown Beirut was expropriated by Solidere wrote an open letter protesting the destruction of archaeological sites and calling it hyperbolically "the crime of the twentieth century"; see *al-Hayat*, September 21, 1995.

[11] Other examples of Christian areas targeted by Hariri for disfigurement include the town of Hadath south of Beirut, where throughout the summer of 1995 a standoff occurred between government bulldozers and angry residents camping out in the streets over Hariri's plans to create a huge vegetable market in the center of town. The bulldozers eventually retreated. That was not the case in downtown Beirut, where Solidere took advantage of Israel's April 1996 "Operation Grapes of Wrath" to bulldoze seven historical buildings, leading residents to protest with an all-night candlelight vigil on May 3.

Lebanon and beyond. Indeed, in recent years the country has been the stage for intense Shi'a-Sunni competition, not as much between two approaches to Islamicization as a scramble for mid-level administrative posts in the government bureaucracy and the lucrative deals to be made on the side—in other words, dividing up the spoils of political patronage. In this context, Hariri's enormous wealth and autocratic bulldozer politics are perceived as a threat, and Berri has fought tooth-and-nail to secure appointments for his cronies.

Hariri has a decided preference for grandiose schemes and little regard for the cost, particularly if the latter is calculated in cultural or sociological (rather than monetary) currency. He has no qualms with reproducing an amalgamated Hong Kong-Jeddah hybrid in the middle of downtown Beirut and calling it reconstruction. Islamicization may not be deliberate in every instance; Arab and Ottoman archaeological remains were bulldozed along with the rest. But the preferred architectural style is the ornamented, pseudo-native structures that adorn the oil-rich cities of Arabia. Thus, his most vehement opponents see his bombastic reconstruction schemes as embodying a lethal dose of desertification, leading to the obliteration of authentic Lebanese architecture.[12] What hangs in the balance between the roar of bulldozers, the screams of protesters, and the insensitivity of dealmakers are some 4,000 years of cumulative and unparalleled urban history steadily evaporating into the winds of a lost golden opportunity.

ECONOMIC STAGNATION

If Hariri has plenty of detractors, he also has admirers—or, more accurately, self-styled "realists." This group comprises businessmen, corporate executives, and financial analysts from every community, along with the swelling numbers of men and women directly or indirectly on Hariri's payroll. They optimistically maintain that Hariri is first and foremost a businessman who cares only about making money, and as such he is the best—and only—hope for attracting badly-needed foreign investment in the war-ravaged Lebanese economy. His alliance with the Syrians is only tactical, they say, and all talk about Islamicization is nonsense. "What is the practical alternative to Hariri?" is the recurring question on these people's lips. The mounting "hidden" costs to Lebanese

---

[12] In a scathing critical analysis of a proposal approved by the Hariri government for a multi-million dollar seafront complex featuring a huge conference center, two hotels, a commercial mall, and theater, renowned architect Jad Thabet attacked the penchant for fake triumphalist edifices (*à la* Stalin) imported wholesale from the failed, impersonal urban experiments of the Arabian Gulf, which ignore the more congenial national styles that are in keeping with the Mediterranean character of the site. "It is the emptiness of the desert transplanted to the shore of the Mediterranean," Thabet wrote; see *al-Nahar* (weekly supplement), February 3, 1996, p. 9.

civil society of Harirism—including the stagnating (and, in places, deteriorating) economy, strained social order, and steady impoverishment of the populace—are conveniently omitted from the optimists' apologia.

Upon becoming prime minister and finding that foreign capital was not pouring into Lebanon as he had initially anticipated, Hariri resorted to a policy of massive internal borrowing. He did so by issuing Law 117, which offered government treasury bonds at an unprecedented 33 percent interest rate—ignoring the advice of experts who counseled that the only way to avoid runaway inflation and a general monetary breakdown in financing reconstruction and other projects would be to offer shares on the open market.[13] Hariri's idea was to use the bonds to generate quick revenue to maintain excessive levels of wasteful government spending (which included slush funds, kickbacks, and other corrupt practices) and service the burgeoning government debt—to which the bonds themselves would of course contribute.

To assess the Hariri government's economic performance, the figures from the government and independent unions speak for themselves. Estimates of Lebanon's 1994 gross domestic product (GDP) range from $5 billion (according to a leading Beirut bank) to $8 billion (according to the Ministry of Finance).[14] In September 1995, the Lebanese Central Bank estimated the national debt at around $7.3 billion—$1.24 billion in external (foreign) debt and $6.06 billion owed internally.[15] This figure did not include huge government loan guarantees and other items kept off the balance sheet, which make the actual size of the debt probably closer to $9.5–10 billion. Considering that only five years earlier the national debt barely exceeded $1 billion,[16] this represents an enormous leap and an

---

[13] For the figure of 33 percent interest on treasury bonds, see the second report by the Coordination Committee of Lebanon's Unions appearing in *al-Hayat*, September 15, 1995. Georges Vedel, one of France's most celebrated legal and financial experts, advised the Hariri government early on to issue shares rather than bonds, because whereas the former distribute profits and losses evenly among shareholders, bonds constitute a portion of the debt incurred by the government treasury at a fixed interest rate with a limited duration. This information comes from an unpublished, confidential study by Pierre Antoine Boujaber, director of the Bank of Kuwait & the Arab World (Ashrafieh branch) in Beirut (June 1995).

[14] The GDP does not include remittances to Lebanon by Lebanese living abroad. The relation of GDP to gross national product (GNP) is as follows: GNP=GDP plus income accruing to domestic residents from investments abroad, minus income earned in the domestic market accruing to foreigners abroad, over a particular period.

[15] See *al-Diyar*, December 1, 1995. The figures for the external debt during the first half of 1995 actually fluctuate between $1.7 billion (according to the Council for Development and Reconstruction, Hariri's inner circle of top cronies, which factors in contracted projects) and $800 million (according to figures from Lebanon's Central Bank, which are based strictly on granted funds).

[16] This and other relevant economic figures came from the independent Coordination Committee for Lebanon's Unions report, August 19, 1995; see *al-Hayat*, August 20, 1995. The head of Lebanon's General Labor Union, Elias Abu-Rizk, announced in October 1996 that the overall national debt had nearly reached $13 billion; see ibid., October 22, 1996.

exponential rate of increase. In mid-1997, foreign sources estimated Lebanon's public debt at between $11.8 billion and $14.7 billion, the latter also said to be roughly equal to its GDP.[17] Though disparate, these figures indicate that Lebanon's national debt is increasing.

The 1996 draft budget projected debt payments at $1.6 billion—a whopping 40.31 percent of projected expenditures for that year—compared to payments of about $1.3 billion in the 1995 budget.[18] In mid-1995, the government estimated that total spending for 1996 would exceed projected revenues by 37.62 percent. By the end of the year, however, the Ministry of Finance officially conceded that deficit spending would more likely be 48 percent of the budget, and independent financial experts predicted it would exceed 55 percent.[19] These projections belied optimistic government forecasts of a significant increase in revenues from $1.9 billion in 1995 to $2.5 billion in 1996—most of which were to come from exorbitant indirect taxes such as car registration fees, fines for construction violations, increased rates for telephone service and other basic utilities, higher gasoline prices, steeper customs duties on imported goods, and other similar sources.[20]

The statistics outlining estimated expenditures for 1996 reveal the Lebanese government's waste, corruption, and poor and unproductive economic planning. Prime Minister Hariri's office (i.e., staff, entourage, personal security, *et cetera*) alone consumed 16.48 percent of the total 1996 projected budget, compared to just 0.07 percent for the president's office and only 0.74 percent for the parliament. Vital ministries such as agriculture and industry, where the real emphasis on economic growth should lie, were allotted a mere 0.81 percent and 0.05 percent, respectively. Urgently needed areas of attention such as the environment and populations internally dislocated as a result of the war, received equally meager percentages of the proposed budget: the Ministry of the Environment, which ought to direct an environmental clean-up following

---

This figure was corroborated by Lebanese financial expert Ziad K. Abdelnour, managing director of InterBank/Birchall Equities in New York. In an interview with the author in fall 1996, Abdelnour added that it would take at least two decades to undo the damage caused by the mounting debt. By mid-1997, Lebanon's public debt had reached $14.7 billion; see Reuters, July 10, 1997.

[17] The estimates come from "Disgruntled in Lebanon," *Economist*, July 12, 1997, p. 41, and Reuters, July 10, 1997, respectively.

[18] In addition to unwise and misdirected spending, a principal reason for this calamitous debt was the inordinately high-yielding treasury bonds; see a report on the government's 1996 draft budget in *al-Safir*, September 28, 1995. For an English translation of the 1996 draft budget, see the U.S. Foreign Broadcast Information Service—Near East and South Asia (FBIS-NES) December 6, 1995, pp. 36-44. The quoted figures have been converted from Lebanese lira to U.S. dollars. By way of comparison, the interest on the U.S. national debt now consumes almost 17 percent of the federal budget and is regarded as far too high.

[19] Ibid., FBIS, December 6, 1995, p. 36. See also the minister of finance's admission about the expected size of the 1996 budget deficit in *al-Hayat*, December 28, 1995.

[20] *Al-Safir*, September 28, in FBIS, December 6, 1995, p. 36.

fifteen years of war and the illegal entry into the country in the 1980s of an untold number of barrels leaking toxic chemical waste (not to mention the ravages that ever larger stone quarries are perpetrating on Lebanon's shrinking pine canopy) was given 0.15 percent; the Ministry of Displaced Persons' Affairs got a puny 0.17 percent.[21]

At the same time, however, the Ministry of National Defense and the Ministry of Interior—the two government bodies that handle security—were allocated 16.98 percent and 7.81 percent, respectively. There remains little question of how much of this money was spent on enhancing the government's ability to improve law and order, stem crime, protect the frontiers, expand the Lebanese army's security duties to South Lebanon, disarm remaining militias, clamp down on terrorists, and begin to take over security functions from Syrian forces, versus how much of it went toward beefing up the repressive apparatus of the regime in Beirut to enable it to continue harassing and detaining innocent citizens, stifling freedoms, aiding and abetting foreign occupation, and intimidating peaceful opposition.[22]

Even if these percentages, and indeed all the projected figures for 1996, were theoretical—not to say illusory—they nonetheless disclose the Hariri government's true intentions. Promoting economic recovery is certainly not high on the government's list of self-serving priorities. Voices of protest rose from many quarters to complain against the government's economic practices, their adverse social impact, and thinly concealed political intentions. Perhaps the most forceful and significant expression of popular opposition to Haririism came from a variety of independent trade and labor unions, professional associations, and syndicates. In 1995 alone, a series of elections in a number of these unions and associations brought forth new leaders openly vocal about their anti-government stand.

Without exception, all of them hailed in one way or another from the ranks of the nationalist, Aoun-inspired movement and were perceived by the government as "Aounists." There were the elections to the various student councils and organizations on college campuses and in high schools throughout Lebanon. The Aounists won with a landslide, including at institutions in predominantly Muslim areas. Among the most notable were the fall 1995 student council elections at the American University of Beirut, in what used to be referred to as Muslim West Beirut. Discontent with Hariri had pierced through communal and religious

---

[21] On the toxins illegally imported into Lebanon, see Fouad Hamdan, "Waste Trade in the Mediterranean: Toxic Attack against Lebanon" (Malta: Greenpeace Mediterranean Office, 1995).

[22] See table in FBIS, December 6, 1995, pp. 43-44. The projected 1996 budget assigned scant resources to other important ministries, including the Ministries of Water Resources (1.57 percent), Health (3.88 percent), Postage and Telecommunications (.38 percent), Labor (.06 percent), Housing and Cooperatives (.35 percent), Transportation (2.46 percent), Culture and Higher Education (1.57 percent), and Municipal and Rural Affairs (.10 percent).

barriers, and Aoun served as a rallying symbol for defiance against official policies. A similar outcome occurred in elections for presidents of the physicians' syndicate, the lawyers' association, and—most devastatingly for the Hariri government—the union of engineers. This last election produced a highly qualified team of architects and engineers led by 'Aasim Salam, an outspoken critic of Solidere and the author of several books and articles on the reconstruction of downtown Beirut.[23]

Another arena of confrontation with the government has been the General Union of Lebanese Workers, Lebanon's powerful and independent labor federation. The union has repeatedly led the campaign against government corruption and defended workers' rights in the face of growing unemployment, higher prices, an unreliable social safety net, and general official indifference to the welfare of the country's laborers. The government fought back by trying to infiltrate the union leadership and create phony parallel unions to weaken the federation, but to no avail. It then appealed to the Syrians to rein in the labor leaders, but again without much success. Matters came to a head when the union called a general strike in July 1995. Security forces disrupted a downtown rally with the help of Syrian intelligence agents and prohibited further demonstrations. The union's message came across loud and clear, however: any remaining semblance of support for the Hariri government had evaporated completely. In a normal democracy, the government would surely have resigned after such a scathing indictment, but in Syrian-occupied Lebanon, Hariri stayed on. Renewed labor unrest ignited in March 1996 from a combination of sudden price rises and wage freezes. The unreconstructed Hariri government then declared a state of emergency and again outlawed public demonstrations. Hariri made a series of quick trips to Damascus to secure approval for his hard-line measures.

In early 1997, the government flagrantly rigged the union's elections and succeeded in getting its "puppet" candidate elected president of the union. When the very popular incumbent president, Elias Abu-Rizk, refused to accept the results, the authorities promptly arrested him and detained him for a week. Despite an outpouring of public sympathy and support for Abu-Rizk, the government refused to repudiate its electoral manipulation and recognize him as the legitimate federation president.

Many months earlier, the theme of government corruption had begun to catch on. Accusations of greed and mafia-style practices were leveled at the government in a manifesto signed by a group of fifty-five intellectuals and published toward the end of 1994. A similarly damning proclamation

---

[23] Salam and a number of other experts are co-authors of *I'mar Bayrut wal Fursa Da'i'ah* (see footnote 4). He also published *Al-i'mar wal Maslaha Al-'aama: Fi Al'amara wal Madina* (*Reconstruction and the Public Interest: On the Building and the City*) (Beirut: Dar Al-Jadid Publishing House, 1995). On the backgrounds and common opposition to government policies of the presidents of the three main associations (for physicians, lawyers, and engineers), see *al-Hayat*, December 17, 1995, which refers to them as "the Three Musketeers of the Lebanese civil opposition."

signed by 150 intellectuals and professionals appeared six months later in the newspapers. The signatories picked up the first group's call for greater transparency in government policies and accountability before the law and the people. They appealed for solidarity with the various trade and professional unions and student groups that had been openly critical of the government on a number of occasions.

They drew particular attention to the need for public scrutiny of financial agencies such as the social security fund, Hariri's Council for Development and Reconstruction, a fund for displaced people (controlled by Druze leader and Minister of the Displaced Walid Jumblat), and the fund for the Council of the South (controlled by Shi'a House Speaker Nabih Berri).[24] It is an open secret that considerable financial abuse goes on in these agencies. Another example is the "side deals" struck between private petroleum companies and the Ministry of Industry and Oil, resulting in some $150 million being diverted annually to a few officials and their sons who conveniently "represent" these companies.[25] Government corruption and the intermingling of private and public interests, long an unfortunate feature of Lebanese politics, have reached epidemic proportions under Hariri.

This issue of government corruption resonated poignantly with an already disaffected electorate during the summer 1996 parliamentary elections. Elias Abu-Rizk, putative head of the independent labor union and a bitter critic of the Hariri government, ran as an independent in the parliamentary elections in his home district in the south. In one sense, these contrived elections pitted a puritanical, even sanctimonious extremism spearheaded by Hezbollah against a corrupt and generally complacent moderation as represented by Hariri and his allies. Although Abu-Rizk did not win, he managed to garner an impressive 96,000 protest votes from people seething with anger against a set of overburdening measures and regulations imposed by an otherwise insensitive and unscrupulous government. He even received Hezbollah support in the process because of his anti-government positions.

Widespread abuses by government officials before and since the elections, combined with mounting indirect taxation, galloping inflation, soaring unemployment, and a still shoddy infrastructure have nearly wiped out the country's middle class and swelled the ranks of the impoverished. From the vantage point of this large and growing mass of people, talk of economic recovery and reconstruction offers little solace in the face of everyday hardships. The minimum monthly wage hovers around $100, while prices for many basic commodities are comparable to those in Europe's most expensive cities or the oil-rich Gulf states. The purchasing power of people with low and fixed incomes has declined 80 percent since

---

[24] See *al-Hayat*, December 9, 1994 and June 10, 1995.

[25] For an article exposing the officials and private companies involved in this scandal and providing exact figures for the illegal deals concluded, see *al-Anwar*, July 16, 1995.

1984. Unemployment in 1995 was over 32 percent and rising,[26] as cheap foreign labor flooded the Lebanese market. The exodus of skill and talent from the country continues despite all the reassurances about the imminent recovery. School tuitions are going through the roof trying to keep up with inflation, yet very little money was allocated in the 1996 budget for improving the public education sector. Hariri's version of austerity measures as part of his stringent fiscal policy included resisting significant wage increases in the public domain while piling up revenues through unpopular indirect taxes.[27]

THE SYRIAN ECONOMIC BONANZA

While "security and stability" remains their main alibi for staying in Lebanon, the Syrians are having a field day in the country's economic mayhem. For the first time, the hard currency exiting Lebanon at the hands of Syrian workers and other Syrians exceeds the amount being remitted back to Lebanon by Lebanese working abroad. The one million or so Syrian workers throughout Lebanon earned around $15 million a day, of which barely $3 million is being spent in the country. The bulk of the remainder is being transferred out of Lebanon at the rate of $300 million every month or $3.6 billion annually.[28] In effect, Lebanon—which at one time thrived on the remittances of citizens living and working overseas (Shi'a in Africa, Sunnis in the Gulf, and Christians everywhere)—has now become the source of a growing remittance economy for Syria. The damage this hard currency drain is having on the battered Lebanese economy is not difficult to imagine. As dollars become more scarce, demand for them rises, which in turn subjects the Lebanese lira to downward devaluationary pressure. In the face of this adverse development, the government's strategy has been for the Central Bank to intervene artificially and "rescue" the lira temporarily by using dollars and purchasing lira. This futile measure quickly becomes a spiraling vicious circle that squeezes the rest of the economy and the population for more dollars, and the problem is ultimately compounded.

Lebanon's economy represents much more for the Syrians than a source of hard currency. Virtually every project in Lebanon involves a hidden Syrian partner, usually a member of the ruling elite or the

---

[26] See the two reports by the independent Coordination Committee for Lebanon's Unions, published in *al-Hayat* on August 20 and September 15, 1995, repectively.

[27] Some areas and groups suffered this form of taxation more than others. Whereas the government was able to collect increased fees for basic utilities from the Christian areas, for example, in Beirut's southern (mostly Shi'a) suburbs people continued to illegally tap into public electricity poles and obtain free power as the government looked the other way.

[28] These figures are from an unpublished June 1995 study by Lebanese economist Pierre Antoine Boujaber of the Bank of Kuwait & the Arab World (Ashrafieh branch) in Beirut; see footnote 16.

intelligence and security apparatus. As a result, the cost of getting anything done in Lebanon has gone up.[29] Moreover, the sheer weight of Syria's influence in the country compels Solidere and others to give preference to Syrian contractors, maintenance crews, suppliers of raw materials, and freight truckers over local or foreign competitors. The Syrians are entangled in rackets of every variety: vegetables, cigarettes, automobiles, cement, clothes, gasoline, fertilizers, and more. Their agents regularly canvass the streets of Beirut knocking on the doors of large companies and private businesses in order to solicit subscriptions to the official Syrian newspapers and organs of the regime. Fearing the consequences if they do not comply with this form of extortion, many of the targeted companies and businesses give in. Drug trafficking and counterfeiting are two other revenue-generating activities that the Syrians supervise in Lebanon. The notorious counterfeit hundred-dollar bill referred to as the "Supernote," a major headache for the U.S. Treasury Department and Secret Service, originates somewhere in Lebanon or Syria, and is manufactured with the full knowledge and acquiescence of Syrian authorities.[30]

Having become increasingly tied to the Lebanese economy—and the ill-gotten benefits therefrom—while remaining oblivious to the negative repercussions of their actions, the Syrians have no intention of quitting Lebanon anytime soon. There have even been intriguing suggestions that Lebanon could eventually serve more or less the same role for Syria as Hong Kong does for China.[31] The trend in the world economy toward free trade, open markets, increased privatization, and global integration is undoubtedly having a growing impact on the Middle East. Centralized, Soviet-style command economies such as Syria's are obsolete and will have to undergo radical transformation in the near future to remain viable.

The Lebanese mercantile spirit has already begun to contaminate influential individuals in the Syrian ruling hierarchy and the military. There are modest signs of liberalization in the Syrian economy and, as the

---

[29] See John Battersby, "Why Lebanon Follows the Road to Damascus," *Christian Science Monitor*, August 1, 1995, p. 6. Though informative, Battersby's article suffers from a familiar slew of inaccuracies: Lebanon after World War I was *not* "carved" or "excised" from Syria, a then presumed coherent political entity, and Hariri has *not* "managed to win significant support among the Christian elite," but merely succeeded in buying a few unrepresentative voices here and there.

[30] On the "Syrian connection" in drug trafficking out of Lebanon, see "The Lebanese Inferno: Drugs and Terror," in Rachel Ehrenfeld, *Narco-Terrorism: How Governments Around the World Used the Drug Trade to Finance and Further Terrorist Activities* (New York: Basic Books, 1990), pp. 52-73. On Syria and the "Supernote," see Fredric Dannen and Ira Silverman, "The Supernote," *New Yorker*, October 23, 1995, pp. 50-55. See also "Iran, Syria Still Flood Mideast With Forgeries," Compass News Service, October 18, 1995. According to the Compass report, deutschmarks, Saudi Arabian riyals, and United Arab Emirates dirhams were being forged in addition to U.S. hundred-dollar bills. For an updated account of Syrian involvement in drugs and counterfeiting in Lebanon, see "Syria's Game: Both Ends Against the Middle," *New York Times*, June 15, 1996.

[31] Battersby, "Why Lebanon Follows the Road to Damascus."

region moves inexorably toward peace, many of these changes could become permanent.[32] Allowed to flourish unhampered, Lebanon's strong tradition of free market economics can play a crucial role in this regard. Yet paradoxically, the longer the Syrians remain in Lebanon, the less either economy will open up. On the contrary, the combination of continued Syrian heavy-handedness and the closed coterie of beneficiaries among the ruling class in Damascus will ensure economic stagnation for both Lebanon and Syria.

Unlike Hong Kong, Lebanon is emerging from a long period of war and devastation. Before helping other countries or serving as an economic role model, Lebanon urgently needs to put its own economic house in order. If counterproductive economic policies of the Hariri government persist, little can be expected of Lebanon's capacity as a *laissez faire* catalyst. There still exists in Lebanon, mainly among the less educated Muslim masses, an ingrained tendency to expect large-scale assistance from the government and shun private initiatives for self-help. The socio-economic messages and appeals in the weekly Friday prayer sermons broadcast from the mosques in Beirut have clear undertones of this socialist streak of a centralizing mentality mingled with dependency on government handouts, both of which breed lethargy and encourage inflated expectations in their audience.[33] To increase the economic dynamism of the Muslim community as a whole to the level of the Christians, Lebanon requires a prolonged recuperative period during which the monopolistic and otherwise detrimental practices of Hariri and his cohorts give way to greater decentralization and privatization, and the deadweight of Syrian occupation gradually recedes. As this seems too much to expect anytime soon, the Hong Kong analogy clearly does not apply in the case of Lebanon and Syria.[34]

Many observers predict excellent long-range economic prospects for Lebanon in the wake of a comprehensive Middle East peace. In a New Year's Day interview in 1996, Hariri confidently declared that Lebanon after peace "will be a financial, commercial, cultural, and tourism center in the region."[35] Yet Hariri's "rhetorical" economic predictions hardly harmonize with the realities of his "one-man show" approach. Prior to

---

[32] The best example of this is Syria's May 1991 Investment Law no. 10, which allowed greater freedom of investment for the private sector, eased the regulations for capital transfer, and encouraged foreign investment by providing incentives and lifting certain restrictions; see Sylvia Poelling, "Investment Law no. 10: Which Future for the Private Sector?," in ed. Eberhard Kienle, *Contemporary Syria: Liberalization Between Cold War and Cold Peace* (London: British Academic Press & the University of London, 1994), pp. 14-25.

[33] This is not to imply that all Muslims fall into this category. There are some highly enterprising and successful Muslims in Lebanon, just as there are lazy and parasitic elements among the Christians. Only broad trends are described here.

[34] Ironically, the analogy may still apply but in an obverse way. If over time Hong Kong becomes indistinguishable from Shanghai or any other large Chinese city and the present trend of Syrian absorption continues in Lebanon, an analogy could indeed be made.

[35] See *al-Nahar*, January 1, 1996.

Israel's Operation Grapes of Wrath in April 1996, he relied on the narcotic effect that the mere *anticipation* of economic prosperity, buttressed by erratic spurts of spot improvements, had on the public. This kind of economic "smoke and mirrors" no longer applies. Hariri and those around him need to realize that much of the economic thinking in Lebanon is retrograde and outdated. Insularity, excessive secrecy, monopolistic cliquishness, resistance to change, obsession with short-term profits, and devotion to the myth of the indispensable middleman are sure recipes for stagnation. Until these policies are identified as a major part of the problem, all talk of impending prosperity will remain hollow.

More concretely, serious foreign investors need a state-of-the-art telecommunications infrastructure and less overall opacity in the system. Lebanon's telecommunications remains in deplorable condition more than four years after Hariri took office. Much of the computer technology in Lebanon resides in the entertainment, rather than economic, sector. As a result, the country is information-poor and the gap with the developed world is widening. Over time, the Lebanese are realizing that they cannot compete or attract investment if the current trend continues. Of course, from the Syrian perspective, there is little reason to allow an occupied country to be too easily linked to the outside world.

Expectations of economic improvements were also greatly dampened following the May 1996 change of government in Israel and the overall deceleration of the peace process. Any future acceleration would bring Shimon Peres' optimistic vision of a "new Middle East" much closer to realization.[36] Yet Syrian-occupied and Hariri-ravaged Lebanon will be left behind when the inevitable "jump start" to the peace process kicks in. Once the region leaps ahead in an era of peace, Lebanon will have an enormous amount of catching up to do. There is the real danger that it may be losing much of its qualitative edge on the human level, and will eventually sink into a regional backwater. Beirut's refusal to participate in the series of Middle East/North Africa economic summits (in Casablanca in 1994, Amman in 1995, and Cairo in 1996) was a bad omen for the future. Political considerations were obviously the deciding factor, as they have been with Lebanon's official absence from the multilateral peace talks, but no attempt was made even to have a "back channel" presence or at least be cognizant of looming economic prospects and opportunities at the economic conference.

A proper reconstruction strategy requires being poised to take advantage of the newly emerging opportunities whenever and wherever they arise. It also means a genuine effort to broaden the spectrum of citizen participation in the reconstruction process on every level, rather than concentrating it in the hands of a few at the top.[37] Just as party

---

[36] See Shimon Peres, *The New Middle East* (New York: Henry Holt & Company, 1995).

[37] See Bayhum, *Reconstruction and the Public Interest*. Among other things, Bayhum suggests that the government offer loans to small- and medium-sized businesses instead of relying

officials and *apparatchiks* emerged to form the new capitalist elite after the collapse of communism in the states of Eastern Europe, the warlords and militia chiefs in Lebanon became government ministers and, with Hariri, appear to be dividing the spoils among them. If the 1996 parliamentary elections revealed a trend in the flawed world of Lebanese politics, it was the emergence of a plutocratic class of "the people's representatives." This situation is creating islands of the "super rich" among vast expanses of the poor, who feel excluded and voiceless in the rebuilding of their own capital and country.

---

exclusively on imported capital from the Persian Gulf Arab states. He also notes that internal financial, legal, and bureaucratic reforms; enhanced transparency and availability of data for public scrutiny; and more informed public debate on issues pertaining to reconstruction are long overdue in Lebanon. For a review of the book, see *al-Hayat*, December 17, 1995. See also the article by Hazim Saghieh in ibid., September 28, 1996, in which he points out Hariri's error of proceeding with reconstruction while continuing to politically and economically marginalize the Christians.

IV

Civil Society Fights Back

On several fronts along the active demarcation lines in the new phase of confrontation in Lebanon, civil opposition is putting up stiff resistance to the status quo being created and sustained by the Beirut authorities and those behind them. The ultimate fate of Lebanon will be decided more on these fronts than at any negotiating table or backroom deal. In addition to downtown property owners, those concerned with archaeology, and independent unions, those waging the battle include newspaper editors and television station managers, teachers and school directors, parents and students, some courageous lawyers and judges with integrity, non-governmental human rights organizations, and the many informal ad hoc gatherings of citizens worried about their and their children's futures. The disparate individuals and groups that comprise this loose and amorphous opposition span Lebanon's communal spectrum and, though occasionally concentrated more in some quarters than others, they all have one thing in common: They have seen the face of free Lebanon as they had known it savagely altered before their eyes, and they don't like what they see.

THE MEDIA

It is difficult to imagine Lebanon without a free press. At the turn of the century, the Arab world saw the birth of modern newspapers and magazines in Beirut and Cairo. Since mid-century the thriving and privately owned free press in Beirut has been unmatched by Middle East standards in its vigilance over elected officials and campaign for public accountability. Although the military regimes of the Arab world were occasionally successful in extending their influence to some of Beirut's newspapers, where specific editors (and thus their publications) landed on a foreign payroll, the Lebanese press by and large managed to preserve its considerable freedom and remain in private hands.

During the long years of the Lebanon war, a veritable electronic revolution was taking place around the world, particularly in the fields of computers and telecommunications. The various warring militias hastened to acquire audio-visual media capabilities in the form of their own private radio and television stations, which they used effectively for propaganda and military purposes. Despite the tensions and hatreds these duels on the airwaves fueled, there was a positive outcome for the country: broadcasting skills were honed, technical sophistication was achieved, and most important of all, freedom of expression was safeguarded even in the blackness of war. These developments would have been impossible had the ingrained regional conception of the media as a forum for perpetual flattery of the ruling regime prevailed.

Open intimidation of the press commenced when the Syrians first arrived on the Lebanese scene. In 1980, Riyad Taha, president of the Association of Lebanese Journalists, was assassinated. He had been openly unsympathetic to the Syrians and maintained links with the rival Iraqi Ba'th. That same year Salim Lawzi, editor-in-chief of *al-Hawadeth* magazine, was tortured and executed for allegedly insulting President Assad. Both were prominent Lebanese and Arab journalists, and both were Muslims. Their brutal deaths initially terrorized the Lebanese media, and the intimidating aftereffects never quite wore off. After Taif, the shaky justification for increased censorship offered by the Beirut authorities was that it helped to advance national reconciliation by curbing inflammatory or sectarian outbursts. In addition, Article 12 of the August 1991 Syrian-Lebanese "Defense and Security Agreement" prohibits "all military, security, political, and *media* activity that might harm" either country.[1]

Since 1992, the Beirut authorities have repeatedly attempted to subjugate and tame the country's free media. Relying on a regrettable clause in the Taif agreement that requires all audio-visual and printed media to conform with the law and the principle of responsible freedom "in the service of orientation toward reconciliation," the authorities embarked on a campaign to silence and then streamline Lebanon's print, radio, and television media to reflect the government's policy. When some newspapers and television stations acted defiantly or objected to these intrusive government measures, they were promptly closed down and their managers taken to court. In a move underscoring its intolerance for dissent, in a one month span in 1993 the Lebanese government shut down four independent news organizations and filed criminal charges against four journalists for violating Lebanon's restrictive new press and broadcast regulations. The severe action was reminiscent of the newly-arrived Syrian forces forcible closure of five Beirut newspapers in 1976.[2]

One outspoken anti-government television station was closed down and accused of fomenting sectarian strife by reporting on Hariri's alleged plan to "Islamize" Lebanon. According to the Human Rights Watch, there was ample evidence to suggest that the real reason was the station's regular airing of views in political opposition to both the Lebanese and Syrian governments.[3] In addition, three leading Beirut dailies were closed and

---

[1] Italics added; see *al-Nahar*, September 7, 1991.

[2] For a full account of the unprecedented Lebanese government crackdown on the country's news media, see Human Rights Watch/Middle East, "Lebanon's Lively Press Faces Worst Crackdown Since 1976" (New York: July 1993).

[3] Ibid., p. 3.

legal proceedings initiated against their publishers. These included the right-wing *Nida' al-Watan*, charged with violations similar to those of the television station, and the openly pro-Syrian *al-Sharq*, for displaying a cartoon deemed insulting to President Hrawi and his family.[4]

The influential left-of-center and normally pro-Syrian daily *al-Safir* was closed ostensibly for publishing an Israeli draft proposal presented at the Middle East peace negotiations then being held in Washington.[5] The reaction to the closure was swift and widespread, with a large number of prominent Lebanese newspaper editors, heads of syndicates, members of parliament, and even members of Hariri's own cabinet vigorously protesting the government move. The huge outcry and threat of an open-ended strike by the guild of editors and journalists eventually led the government to back down. The charges against the publishers were dropped and *al-Safir* resumed publication eight days after it was shut down. Similarly, *Nida' al-Watan* was eventually permitted to reopen.

The showdown with the recalcitrant media did not end with the closure episode. Following a February 1994 explosion (attributed to the Christian Lebanese Forces militia) in a church north of Beirut, the minister of information issued a decree banning all radio and television news broadcasts and political commentary.[6] The only exception was Hezbollah's radio and television stations, which continued to broadcast news and political programs under the pretext of being legitimate resistance to the Israeli occupation of southern Lebanon. The ban was soon expanded to encompass specific patriotic songs and theatrical plays considered provocative. This unwarranted assault on culture and civil liberties in the name of "public order" met severe opposition.

The protests grew louder when the cabinet invoked Decree 104 (of June 1977), which gave the government wide-ranging authority to shut down and confiscate publications that insult the president and other prominent officials or that commit offenses specified by the decree and related laws. Publishers and editors of delinquent papers were now threatened with imprisonment and heavy fines. The wave of complaints against these arbitrary government measures swelled: thirty-eight members of parliament signed a petition calling for "respect for human rights and civil liberties, in particular political freedoms, freedom of information, and

---

[4] Due to *al-Sharq*'s close ties to Syria, the closure was rescinded two days later; see ibid., pp. 21-22.

[5] Ibid., p. 19. The real reason, according to the editor-in-chief, had to do with the paper's critical coverage of Saudi Arabia.

[6] A Ministry of Information serves no useful or constructive purpose and has to be viewed as an unnecessary vestige of authoritarianism and centralized control. No self-respecting democracy has a ministry devoted solely to media matters, let alone to "regulating" public information. Freedom of expression and opinion is sacred in all civilized and open societies, and the full autonomy of the media is respected because it is expected to maintain a vigilant watchful eye on the performance of public officials. Although Lebanon had a Ministry of Information prior to Syrian entry, it was generally benign and far less intrusive. This is no longer the case.

freedom for the syndicates."[7] The representative of the Committee for the Defense of Press Freedoms in Lebanon wrote that "it is the Arab regimes that need to progress toward the openness of Lebanon, not Lebanon that must imitate them and acquire their reactionary politics, retrograde ideology, and monolithic way of thinking."[8]

In the end, the government gave in to public pressure and scrapped the draconian powers it had assumed under Decree 104. Official censorship of publications remained, however, and the ban on passing out leaflets, putting up political posters, and radio and television news broadcasts continued. After almost six months, the ban on news was finally lifted in July 1994. Yet what viewers saw when the news programs resumed was a scared and tamed media. Self-censorship—unprecedented for Lebanon's free and habitually irreverent press—had become the order of the day. The authorities had succeeded in instilling an internalized control mechanism within every publication and news broadcast, a mechanism that operated spontaneously on the principle of fear.

Despite the stifling government restrictions and an appalling degree of fear-induced self-censorship, Lebanon's media remain only partially muzzled, with plenty of subtle criticism and unflattering commentary about the government available to the discerning consumer.[9] For exactly this reason, in January 1996 the authorities renewed their assault on the media, specifically independently owned and operated television stations. Using the pretext that there were too many stations broadcasting within a relatively small area, the government issued a "technical report" recommending that Lebanon's more than fifty stations be reduced to six. It had begun to draft what came to be known as "the law to unify the media" when a curious revelation surfaced: five of the six stations selected to continue operating turned out to be owned (or largely controlled) by the senior government officials; the sixth was controlled by Hezbollah.[10]

---

[7] For details on this confrontation and overall government restrictions on the media, see the report (in Arabic) by the independent Beirut-based Foundation for Human and Humanitarian Rights/Lebanon (FHHR/L) entitled *Annual Report for 1994* (Beirut, 1995), pp. 19-28. On Decree 104, see *Annual Report*, pp. 38-39. For an analysis of the report, see *al-Nahar*, December 14, 1995.

[8] Ibid.

[9] One example of media defiance in the face of government pressure is *al-Nahar* (weekly supplement), December 6, 1995. The edition coincided with International Human Rights Day (December 10), which celebrates the anniversary of the Universal Declaration of Human Rights. The entire, twenty-three page edition was devoted to human rights in Lebanon and was vehemently critical of the Beirut government's numerous offenses in this regard. Since then, it has become standard practice for *al-Nahar* to issue a monthly supplement devoted exclusively to what it designates "People's Rights." Gibran Tueini, the editor in charge of the newspaper's weekly supplement and weekly section for youth, demonstrated great courage throughout 1996 by being outspokenly candid in his attacks on both the Beirut government and Syrian practices in Lebanon.

[10] The stations and their owners are Télé-Liban (government-run), Future TV (Prime Minister Hariri), M-TV (Minister of Interior Michel Murr), NBN TV (Speaker of Parliament

In a wave of public protest, leading union, parliamentary, and religious figures representing every Lebanese community deplored both the forced streamlining of broadcast outlets (resulting in an "official" version of events) and their obscene monopolization by the ruling clique. Even Hezbollah officials joined in "as a matter of principle" to defend the right of every group to have its say.[11] A November 30 deadline for consolidation passed without incident. In June 1997, the government authorized the London-based and Saudi-owned MBC to operate in Lebanon. The following month, it officially recognized Hezbollah's television and radio stations. As of mid-1997, the controversy and heated showdown over the other independent stations remained unresolved.

With the onset in April 1996 of Israel's "Operation Grapes of Wrath" against Hezbollah, the country's media were enlisted in the propaganda war directed at "the Zionist aggressor." This exercise was intended to reflect the government's much-touted spirit of "national unity" and the "cohesiveness" of Lebanon's communities in the face of an external threat.[12] Following the deaths of over 100 Lebanese Shi'a civilians when Israel shelled the UN compound in the southern village of Qana on April 18, Lebanon's diverse media chimed in a coordinated chorus of condemnation, lamentation, and anger. Suddenly, it made sense from the Syrian perspective to have as many media voices as possible raised in

---

Berri), Lebanese Broadcasting Corporation (major shareholders include pro-Syrian Suleiman Franjieh, Jr. and millionaire Issam Fares), and al-Manar (Hezbollah).

[11] Throughout early 1996, the leading Beirut dailies featured continuous reports and statements from the government and opposition coalition on the issue of television broadcasts and media streamlining. For a day-by-day account, see the FHHR/L monthly reports for January and February 1996, particularly the summary (pp. 2-3) in each issue.

[12] Using the state-run and -influenced media, the authorities painted a rosy picture of intercommunal harmony and solidarity. They promoted propaganda depicting idyllic images of Christians opening their homes and churches to receive Shi'a refugees fleeing Israeli bombing of their villages in the south. Christians did display great hospitality by taking in hundreds of such refugees, but the reality on the ground was anything but harmonious, however. An unpublished study by a group of independent Lebanese reporters and human rights activists documented a series of incidents revealing acute communal and religious friction—precipitated mainly by repeated provocations on the part of Hezbollah fighters and incompatible religious outlooks and practices.

Attempts by armed Hezbollah fighters to place banners, posters, and even anti-aircraft guns (to shoot at Israeli aircraft) in Christian areas, for example, were angrily repulsed by residents, and the army had to intervene to avert violent confrontations between the two sides. Armed Hezbollahis driving around Christian neighborhoods waving weapons and blaring propaganda from loudspeakers were similarly driven off by enraged residents.

Meanwhile, some of the Shi'a refugees in one Christian village audaciously complained about the church bells being too loud during Sunday church services—and were promptly asked to leave. In another incident, a group of Shi'a refugees refused to accept food from their Christian hosts because it had not been prepared according to Islamic strictures. The village officials expected the *sheikh* accompanying the refugees to issue a religious ruling allowing for an exception under dire circumstances (thereby contributing to the alleged spirit of intercommunal solidarity and national unity); when this did not happen, they asked the refugees to depart at once.

harmonious denunciation of Israel's actions in Lebanon. The notion of reducing and regulating Lebanon's media was temporarily suspended.

As preparations for parliamentary elections continued through that summer, the authorities deemed it useful to retain an assortment of "independent" radio and television channels in order to convey the impression of free debate. The government was so confident during the five-week election period that it did little to curb the wave of wall posters protesting the holding of elections under Syrian tutelage or to disrupt a series of public rallies organized by the opposition (although it did impose a strict news blackout on any reporting about the rallies). The day after the last round of elections, however, the government issued a decree ordering the closure of all television and radio stations except the official government station and the four others belonging to the country's top ruling figures.[13] (Hezbollah was later officially allowed to keep its broadcasting facilities.) All other stations were ordered to cease news broadcasts immediately pending final closure on November 30. The resultant protests referred to these measures as an "information massacre," which threatened to "unemploy" nearly 10,000 journalists, artists, critics, broadcasters, editors, directors, and workers.[14]

The Lebanese government reacted with callous disregard to accusations that it was curtailing free speech. On the eve of Hariri's October 1996 visit to Washington, the prestigious New York-based Committee to Protect Journalists (CPJ) appealed to the Lebanese prime minister to drop libel charges against three Lebanese journalists working for the *al-Diyar* newspaper (which often features opposition views) who had published articles and a cartoon deemed irreverent by the government and faced up to two years in prison and steep fines for their alleged offenses. In a strongly worded letter to Hariri, the CPJ complained that "such measures represent clear violations of the right to 'seek, receive, and impart information and ideas through any media and regardless of frontiers,' guaranteed by Article 19 of the Universal Declaration of Human Rights." Hariri, who was preoccupied at the time with securing his "photo opportunity" with President Clinton, simply ignored the letter.[15]

---

[13] See *al-Nahar*, September 18, 1996. The crackdown on Lebanon's media was also reported in the foreign press; see, for example, "Lebanon Curb on Political Broadcasting," *Financial Times*, September 19, 1996.

[14] See an unpublished letter dated September 24, 1996 by Tahseen Khayyat, head of the New Television station, addressed on behalf of the Follow-up Committee of the Audio-Visual Media in Lebanon to U.S. senators and representatives; see also an editorial by Sarkis Naoum in *al-Wasat*, no. 246 (October 14, 1996); and "Media Muzzle in Lebanon May be Mideast Power Play," *Christian Science Monitor*, October 21, 1996.

[15] For more on the letter from the CPJ to Prime Minister Rafiq Hariri, see *Attacks on the Press in 1996* (New York: CPJ, 1997). A copy of the letter was also sent to President Clinton.

EDUCATION

In Lebanon, 68 percent of all education occurs in private Christian, Muslim, and secular schools. Of these, around 31 percent are Catholic, and the remaining 37 percent are Greek Orthodox, Protestant, secular, Sunni, Shi'a, and Druze. Many Muslim children study at private Christian schools; the reverse, however, is rare. Surprisingly throughout the war years, some Catholic schools grew and spread in Muslim areas such as West Beirut and predominantly Shi'a Nabatiyyeh in the south. In largely Sunni Tripoli in the north, Greek Orthodox schools are thriving. Between 1992 and 1994, the minister of education issued permits for some 140 new Islamic schools, run by both Sunni (a consortium of northern Lebanese fundamentalists) and Shi'a. The authorities have since closed some of them on the grounds that they were fomenting religious intolerance.

The idea of making Arabic the single mandatory language of instruction in Lebanese schools—in other words, "Arabizing" Lebanon's educational curricula—is not a new one. The notion was raised inconclusively on several occasions prior to the 1975 outbreak of war in Lebanon, usually by ideological Arabists, Arab nationalists, or extremist Islamists, all of whom somehow saw in Lebanon's multilingualism and multiculturalism a betrayal of the country's "Arab identity." The Christians always fiercely opposed the idea, arguing that it represented a combination of unacceptable Islamicization and a regressive step toward cultural impoverishment. With a strong tradition of private education (based primarily on Catholic and other Christian religious schools), Lebanon had successfully resisted previous calls for Arabization.

In an effort to consolidate their October 1990 takeover of Lebanon, the Syrians—through their Lebanese surrogates—revived the issue of Arabization. In November of that year, the Beirut government issued Decree 29, which compelled Lebanon to adhere to the charter of the Arab Organization for Education, Culture, and the Sciences established in 1964. Article 12 of the charter, for example, urges Arab states to adopt a "mother textbook" as the standard reference for all study of Arab history, geography, language, and literature. In conjunction with this, the Lebanese Ministry of Education proposed a standardized history textbook exhibiting a definite slant in favor of the country's alleged "Arab" identity. Because the word "Arab" is synonymous with "Islamic" in the charter, Lebanon's Christians were strongly opposed to it.[16] When word got out that the organization's charter calls for Arabizing school curricula, an outcry ensued among the country's powerful private religious schools, which vowed to defy any such measure.

---

[16] Indeed, the charter's call for eventual Arab cultural unity would be detrimental to Lebanon's inherent pluralism and diversity. Moreover, Articles 8 and 15 provoke Christian fears of Islamicization by stipulating, respectively, that future generations be raised "on the principles of religion," and that member countries cooperate to revive and propagate "Arab Islamic culture." In this context, "religion" obviously means Islam.

Moreover, an imposed monolithic interpretation of Lebanese history ignores the fact that the country is essentially a composite society. In such instances, the best way to proceed—short of permitting a plethora of differing accounts of the same events presented in separate books (which is not necessarily a bad idea)—would be to produce a single work that offers the wide and even conflicting spectrum of views and interpretations on controversial issues or events that the various communities and subgroups of Lebanon espouse, along with whatever credible scholarly substantiation or refutation of these views is available. Instead of acknowledging Lebanon's healthy diversity and protecting the freedom of thought and opinion by allowing individual pupils to formulate their definitive interpretations and final conclusions, the authorities at the Ministry of Education intend to impose a politically motivated assimilationist version of history designed to obliterate real differences in the name of an artificial Arab-Islamic supra-identity. As long as Lebanon's private educational sector remains strong and resolute, however, Beirut will find it very difficult to enforce this writ.[17]

But perhaps the single greatest cause of acrimony was Article 10, which declares: "The member countries agree that Arabic will be the language of teaching and research at all levels of education." The cultures that are currently producing most of the scientific breakthroughs and discoveries speak English, French, German, Russian, and Japanese. Limiting Lebanese students to Arabic textbooks would be tantamount to a return to ignorance and stagnation. Such a proposal clearly aims to extinguish the flame of liberal education, openness to the outside world, and Lebanon's qualitative regional edge in the realm of education. Ideologizing and regimenting the process of education poisons any climate of free thought, inquiry, and creativity. Only totalitarianism is served. No privately run pedagogic institution of good reputation will stand for it. If it is allowed to continue, state interference in education will yield the unfortunate experiences of the Soviet Union, fascist Italy, and Nazi Germany: drab uniformity and indoctrination resulting in intellectual sterility and culminating in atrocities. Arab culture already suffers from an excess of these features, and Arab governments should seek to emulate Lebanon's progressive liberal system of education, not the reverse.

Realizing that this abrasive approach was not yielding the desired results, the Beirut authorities altered their strategy and resorted to economic pressure. When the fighting in Lebanon ended and schools began to return to their normal duties and schedules, many of the

---

[17] For more on the Arab organization's charter and adverse local reactions to it, see Habib Malik, "Lebanon in the 1990s," pp. 88-91. For a similar view of the idea of a unified history textbook, see Kamal Salibi, *A House of Many Mansions*, pp. 216-17. Under the pretext of promoting "national assimilation," the Ministry of Education went ahead with plans to produce a unified civics textbook for primary and secondary school students that would presumably inculcate "the strengthening of national awareness." The private schools have already indicated that they will not adopt the government's textbook.

religiously run private schools raised their tuitions to meet higher post-war costs. Since most people still considered government-run schools to be of inferior standards and therefore not a viable option, the public endured the tuition increases and continued to send their children to private schools. The authorities saw this as an opportunity to weaken the private schools and woo public support at the same time. They proposed legislation to freeze tuitions, knowing that this would hurt the already economically strapped schools while receiving enthusiastic public support.

Although the private religious schools do not always see eye-to-eye on educational policies and goals, they did rally together remarkably as soon as they sensed the government onslaught coming. They collectively and summarily rejected the proposed tuition freeze and augmented powers the minister of education sought that would have allowed him, like his counterparts in Syria and Egypt, to fire administrators and principals of private schools at will. The proposed tuition freeze ended up in parliamentary committees on education where it languished and effectively died. Similarly, the government's parallel strategy of advertising cheaper (but inferior) public schools did not pay off in the minds of skeptical parents.

The unified stand among the private schools faltered, however, on the issue of legislating Arabic as the official and sole language of instruction, including in the sciences. The Sunni-run Maqased private schools in and around Beirut continued to support Arabization in education, probably for political and ideological reasons harking back to a latent Nasserism that lingers stubbornly in some quarters. Due to unflinching opposition from Christian and secular schools, the proposal has not been implemented. Nevertheless, the specter of censorship continued to hover over the educational sector, with the authorities attempting to impose it on all schoolbooks prior to their adoption. Once again the private schools put up a fight and the government efforts landed in the oblivion of parliamentary committees. The Ministry of Education did manage to retain veto power over any manuscript of a new schoolbook locally written and produced. Yet in spite of all the hardships and pressures, Lebanon's long tradition of private liberal education has endured and its educational system remains in many respects well ahead of that available in surrounding Arab countries.[18]

ERODING CIVIL RIGHTS

The valiant response by Lebanon's civil society to the mounting challenges and pressures it faces have not arrested the gradual qualitative erosion of its immunity, leading perhaps to irreversible damage. In its 1994

---

[18] The information on education in this section was obtained in an interview with Father Camille Zeidan, director of the Council of Catholic Schools in Lebanon, November 2, 1995.

annual report, one local non-governmental human rights organization posed three telling questions: "Have freedoms in Lebanon, both as theoretical values and an actual reality, become a thing of the past; was the period stretching from 1861 to 1975, when freedoms flourished, an exceptional one; and is the country now reverting back to the regional pattern of oriental despotism?"[19] Though the report points optimistically to tangible indications suggesting the situation is not so desperate, it does not hesitate to present a graphic and sobering account of the widespread infringement of individual and collective rights in Syrian-dominated Lebanon.

Internationally renowned human rights groups have corroborated this assessment of the situation in Lebanon. The section on Lebanon in Amnesty International's 1997 annual report begins, "Scores of possible prisoners of conscience were arrested by the security forces" and goes on to note that "[t]here were continuing allegations of torture and other forms of ill-treatment in custody." The report also indicates that Lebanese government forces and Syrian personnel stationed in Lebanon jointly conducted the arrests.[20] Washington-based Freedom House, which uses an intricate system to sort countries into three basic categories—"free," "partly free," and "not free"—stated in its 1995 report that Lebanon slipped from "partly free" in 1994 to "not free" in 1995 because the country's legislature unilaterally extended the incumbent president's term indefinitely.[21] Freedom House ranked Syria fourteenth among the eighteen most repressive states in the world. At a December 1995 press conference in Washington, Human Rights Watch Executive Director Kenneth Roth criticized the Clinton administration for pursuing the Middle East peace process "as if human rights were irrelevant to it," decrying what he said was "a marked tendency... for the U.S. government to downplay serious human rights abuses in an effort to get everybody around the negotiating table and to secure a peace agreement." He affirmed that Human Rights Watch had been outspoken in its criticism of human rights abuses "in Lebanon and elsewhere without regard to how that might offend the potential negotiating partners such as Syria's Assad."[22]

---

[19] See FHHR/L, *Annual Report for 1994*, p. 58.

[20] See Amnesty International, *Report 1997* (London: Amnesty International, 1997).

[21] See Adrian Karatnycky, "Democracy and Despotism: Bipolarism Renewed?" in *Freedom Review* 27, no. 1 (New York: Freedom House, January-February 1996), pp. 1-21; on Lebanon, see pp. 1, 5, 10, 12. Thirteen specific criteria on Freedom House's checklist of civil liberties were used to rank the world's countries (see pp. 8-9).

[22] Press conference with Kenneth Roth, executive director of Human Rights Watch, held December 7, 1995 at the National Press Club in Washington. In response to questions about Lebanon, Roth called the Clinton administration's neglect of human rights "misguided" because "we believe that a peace founded on ongoing violations of human rights will not be a lasting peace, and that the only way the region can enjoy genuine prosperity and genuine security and peace is when all governments of the region are respectful of human rights." The organization has also been very critical of the grave human rights violations inside Syria

The following year and coinciding with Prime Minister Hariri's October 1996 visit to Washington, Human Rights Watch sent the prime minister an open letter protesting "the abduction of Lebanese citizens and Palestinian refugees in Lebanon by Syrian security forces."[23] She called upon Hariri to take immediate "firm measures" to ensure that the unlawful "disappearances" of civilians come to an end. The letter also noted reports "that Lebanese security forces have participated in the handover of their own citizens to the Syrians, who use torture to elicit information during interrogation." Sherry suggested that Hariri issue a public declaration prohibiting Syrian forces from operating with impunity on Lebanese soil, order the Lebanese judiciary and police to institute procedures for taking written complaints about disappearances, and establish a special legal office to investigate all cases of disappearances "in a prompt and transparent manner."

Needless to say, the letter went unacknowledged and absolutely nothing was done. This is perhaps not surprising, given that the entire process of accusation and detention of suspects is riddled with human rights violations, even by the most elastic standards. Only 10 percent of political cases ever go to trial—let alone reach a verdict. The rest are interminably stalled at the pre-trial detention stage, where most of the abuses are perpetrated. Harassment of defense lawyers by the authorities has become common. Another factor that has contributed to human rights violations in Lebanon in recent years has been the inordinate powers of Lebanon's military court, which was established in 1968 and which has accrued greater power ever since.[24] The very existence of a military court that interferes in civilian legal proceedings under the pretext of a "security threat" is highly problematic; this is compounded by the arbitrary and outrageous extent of its reach. In March 1994, for example, the government-appointed presiding judge boasted that the court had tried 350 cases in a single day—a phenomenal amount considering that the court has only five permanent judges.[25] Little justice or due process could have been meted out at such a pace. In effect, this amounts to the unmistakable "militarization" of the Lebanese judiciary, as more and more civilian cases are tried by the military.

In 1994, President Hrawi announced that "the era of the gallows has arrived."[26] and in the space of five months, four civilians were hanged—compared to only eleven executions in the previous fifty years since Lebanon's independence. In addition to the fundamental ethical questions capital punishment raises, the alacrity with which the trials were

---

itself; see Virginia N. Sherry, *Syria: The Price of Dissent* 7, no. 4 (New York: Human Rights Watch/Middle East, July 1995), along with a fifteen-page summary in Arabic.

[23] See open letter dated October 11, 1996, to Prime Minister Rafiq Hariri from Eric Goldstein, acting executive director of Human Rights Watch/Middle East.

[24] Law No. 24 of April 13, 1968.

[25] FHHR/L *Annual Report for 1994*, p. 12.

[26] Ibid., pp. 15-17.

conducted, verdicts pronounced, appeals denied, and sentences carried out was, to say the least, unsettling. It clearly signaled an underlying political agenda coupled with a calculated show of force by the authorities designed to intimidate any political opposition into submission.

Yet opposition was neither preempted nor silenced. In June 1994, an extraordinary gathering of individuals and groups opposed to the post-Taif status quo in Lebanon took place in Paris. They came from all over the world, including Lebanon itself; the defiant and brave departed from Beirut airport, risking the humiliating treatment some occasionally received at the hands of the security forces and the clear danger that awaited them on the return trip. What came to be known as the Lebanese National Conference was dominated by supporters of Gen. Michel Aoun (who did not personally attend the conference even though he was living in a Paris suburb at the time), but also included many people who simply shared the general's aversion to the ongoing ravages of occupation back in Lebanon. It was the first time in Lebanon's history that such an event had taken place: a kind of opposition "Woodstock-in-exile," the sequel to the heady days in 1989 when the hundreds of thousands camped out around the presidential palace overlooking Beirut when Aoun was its resident.

The conference's final communiqué consisted of a thirteen-page statement that dealt with five specific topics that had been discussed: liberation and freedom in Lebanon, civil liberties and human rights, the Middle East peace process, serious national dialogue and the various constitutional proposals, and reconstruction and the quality of life in postwar Lebanon. It called for the departure of all foreign forces—meaning Israeli and Syrian—from Lebanon, and expressed the desire for "excellent" relations with all Lebanon's neighbors. Also prominent on the list of resolutions were free parliamentary elections and the strengthening of the Lebanese army to enable it to assume full security duties throughout the country. It castigated the government for a poorly conceived reconstruction plan that should have been preceded by the return of the displaced to their villages, the restoration of vital infrastructure, the protection of the archaeological heritage, and greater decentralization to involve more people and broader areas in the actual process of rebuilding.

Not much criticism of the Beirut government emanates from diplomatic circles abroad, mainly because Washington is loathe to say anything that might upset the Syrians, who need to be continuously coaxed to the negotiating table with Israel. One international capital where Lebanon's fortunes continue to matter is the Holy See at the Vatican. The Vatican's Special Synod on Lebanon, held in Rome from November 26 to December 14, 1995, took four years to come to fruition after Pope John Paul II first announced his desire to have such an event. Representatives from all the Christian churches in Lebanon were invited to participate and Muslims were invited as observers. The synod's concluding letter surpassed expectations in its outspokenness on the problems plaguing the country. In addition to reaffirming Lebanon's communal pluralism and cultural diversification, the ecclesiastical document strongly advocated "consensual democracy" in which the majority abide by a communal consensus rather than imposing decisions upon the different sects and denominations that were at variance with their special traditions, values, and belief systems. This was a reaffirmation of the dictum that true democracy is not merely majority rule, but must be coupled with minority rights.

The letter designated Lebanon as belonging culturally to the Arab world, while at the same time being fully open to the rest of the world. Most arresting was a bold call for the departure of both Israeli and Syrian forces. Rarely has an official Vatican-endorsed document been so explicit about Syria's involvement in Lebanon. Other issues raised in the document included the need for adequate affordable housing for newlyweds, less government interference in private education, better salaries for teachers, more attention paid to the impact of economic deterioration on the poor and the middle class, recognition of the pivotal socio-ethical role of the Lebanese family, respect for human rights and the dignity of women, and repatriation of Lebanese abroad and the return of the internally dislocated to their homes.[27] Those who feared that the synod would amount to little more than a "spiritual Taif" and essentially confer its "blessing" on the preceding political agreement were pleasantly surprised by the text of the final letter. On the contrary, the synod drew a clear connection between the success of national reintegration and coexistence, and regaining Lebanese sovereignty. The document's significance will increase as it is carefully examined and appraised on the local parish level.

The infrequency of international scrutiny and publicity emboldens both the Beirut authorities and their Syrian overlords—sometimes to their detriment. In December 1996, for example, an anonymous attack on a Syrian civilian bus in the predominantly Christian area north of Beirut served as a convenient pretext for a wave of arrests that included Wail Kheir, managing director of Lebanon's leading human rights organization, the FHHRL. A local and international outcry ensued, led by lawyers, activists, and renowned human rights organizations abroad. Western diplomats and representatives of the leading democratic nations chimed in with their condemnations of the action. The stunned Beirut authorities were forced to release Kheir and others with apologies. In April 1997, Kheir and a team of human rights activists from Lebanon attended a meeting of the UN Human Rights Committee at UN headquarters in New York to discuss the Lebanese government's compliance with the Covenant on Civil and Political Rights, which it had signed following the 1982 Israeli invasion. The assembled experts issued a scathing indictment of Lebanon's

---

[27] For an English text of the letter, see *Message of the Special Assembly of the Synod of Bishops for Lebanon*, (Vatican City: Catholic Information Center, 1995). For an Arabic translation of the letter, see *al-Hayat*, December 15, 1995. For local reactions (both favorable and critical) to the letter and the synod as a whole, see *al-Hayat*, December 20, 21, and 24, 1995.

dismal human rights record.[28] The Beirut press did not publish the committee's recommendations for three months out of fear of the government's reaction.

Pope John Paul II finally made a long-awaited, two-day pastoral visit to Lebanon in May 1997. Among other things, the event provided interesting demographic information. Unofficial estimates in the Beirut press put the number of participants in the papal Mass at around 700,000 (including a small number of non-Christians). As he made his way to the specially prepared cite for the Mass near the port of Beirut, the Pope passed through another 200,000 cheering Christians lining the streets in the area north of the city; it would have been physically impossible for these people to attend the subsequent Mass. In addition, a number of Christians, including the elderly and very young and many non-Catholics, chose to remain at home and watch the ceremony on television. No matter how these figures are assessed, one thing is clear: the myth—propagated by the Syrians and their local mouthpieces in Lebanon and parroted by some in the West—that the Christians constitute no more than 25-30 percent of Lebanon's population seems to have been shattered. They are much closer to 45 percent, and this refers only to those actually residing in the country. Even the Parliament Speaker Berri conceded on the day of the Pope's Mass that his Shi'a community was not the largest in Lebanon.[29]

---

[28] See *al-Nahar*, June 13, 1997.
[29] See *al-Anwar*, *al-Diyar*, and *al-Nahar*, May 12 and 13, 1997.

V

Lebanon in the Context of a Syria-Israel Peace Agreement

During the November 1995 Euro-Mediterranean summit in Barcelona, Israeli Foreign Minister Ehud Barak happened to be seated at an official luncheon across from Lebanese Foreign Minister Faris Boueiz, whom he did not recognize. In simple Arabic, Barak asked Boueiz what country he was from. Boueiz reportedly glanced in the direction of Syrian Foreign Minister Faruq al-Sharaa, who was sitting two seats away. Realizing that there was only one foreign minister in the room who would look at a Syrian official before responding to such a benign question, Barak muttered, "I guess you are from Lebanon." No less tellingly, Boueiz responded, "More or less." The two men did not speak for the rest of the meal. The fact that Lebanon cannot talk to Israel without Syria's permission sadly sums up Lebanon's pathetic position in its relationship with Syria and the Middle East peace process.[1]

Lebanon is not free to participate meaningfully in shaping its destiny in peace negotiations with Israel. The fact that, in the dynamic and evolving context of Israel-Syria negotiations, Lebanon is almost exclusively seen as a security issue—is indicative of the extent to which it has already been marginalized under the *pax Syriana*. Indeed, its embattled civil society is so preoccupied with defending itself against the corrosive attrition of Syrian occupation, economic deterioration, Islamicization, demographic tampering, and the policies of Rafiq Hariri that it hardly has the luxury of concentrating on the intricate twists and turns of the peace process.

The authorities in the Beirut government and members of parliament do not speak with their own voices, nor do they act on behalf of the Lebanese people and national interests. Thus, a predictable attitude of helpless waiting marks the Lebanese people as they observe how the fate of their country and the future of their children are being decided largely in their absence. The impression has been repeatedly reinforced in their minds that Lebanon is expendable for the sake of achieving a Syrian-Israeli peace deal. Absent such a deal, Lebanon is simply forgotten.

An analysis of Lebanon's place in a potential peace deal between Syria and Israel—and the kind of Lebanon that is likely to emerge after (or in

---

[1] *Jerusalem Post*, November 30, 1995; see also "Ehud Barak: Israel's 'Pragmatic Hawk' Turns Diplomat," *U.S. News & World Report* (December 25, 1995/January 1, 1996), p. 98.

the absence of) such an agreement—requires some general observations about how Syria and Israel define the spectrum of their respective interests in Lebanon. There are three central differences between the Israeli and Syrian presences in Lebanon that will determine to a decisive degree how the "Lebanon factor" plays itself out in the peace negotiations:

• Israel occupies 10 percent of Lebanese territory as its self-declared security zone along its northern border; Syria occupies or effectively controls the remaining 90 percent of Lebanon.

• On more than one occasion, Israel has officially declared that it has no territorial claims on any part of Lebanon and is willing to withdraw completely from southern Lebanon in return for a lasting peace, and has said that it would like a treaty guaranteeing mutual security, diplomatic recognition, an exchange of embassies, and full normalization.[2] Syria, by contrast, has made no official statement about the withdrawal of its forces from Lebanon, and has never had an embassy in Beirut or seen the need for formal diplomatic recognition. On the contrary, official Syrian statements have been about annexing Lebanese territory.[3]

• Whereas Israel exercises no control over the Beirut government, Syria effectively dictates its policies and actions.

An oft-heard quip on the diplomatic peripheries of the peace negotiations—and in Lebanese *salons*—since the 1991 Madrid conference is that Lebanon was not *at* the negotiating table, but *on* it. At the risk of overstretching the metaphor, Lebanon was actually not even on the table, but already in the pocket of one of the parties (Syria) before they entered the negotiating room, with the tacit approval of both Israel and the United States. This anomaly—that Syria's possession of Lebanon goes largely unchallenged—has plagued the Syria-Israel negotiations by reducing

---

[2] There are numerous examples of official Israeli declarations disclaiming any territorial or political ambitions in Lebanon. During an interview on Israel Television on July 29, 1993, then-Foreign Minister Shimon Peres stated "We have no ambitions in Lebanon—neither territorial nor political. . . . [N]ot an inch of Lebanese soil will be taken, not a drop of water." During a visit to the United States later that year, Prime Minister Yitzhak Rabin commented similarly that Israel's "problem with Lebanon is limited to security. . . . We have no territorial [claims in Lebanon and] we do not want one square inch of Lebanese soil or one cubic meter of their water." More recently, in a February 14, 1997 speech at the Washington Institute for Near East Policy, Prime Minister Netanyahu declared that Israel "seek[s] security arrangements that will enable us to withdraw from Lebanon."

[3] A notorious example came in a CNN interview with President Assad broadcast September 28, 1996, in which Assad flatly stated that Lebanon is "an extension" of Syrian territory. At the height of the Lebanon war in 1976, then-Syrian Foreign Minister Abdelhalim Khaddam told the Kuwaiti newspaper *al-Ra'i al-'Aam* (January 7, 1976) that "Lebanon was part of Syria [*sic*], and we shall reclaim it as soon as it actually attempts to split up. It should be made clear that we are referring to the four provinces [Hasbaya, Rashaya, Bekaa, and Baalbek] and not only to the coast, and, furthermore, we are referring also to Mount Lebanon." For the full English text, see Reuven Avi-Ran, *The Syrian Involvement in Lebanon Since 1975* (in Hebrew), trans. David Maisel (Boulder, CO: Westview Press, 1991), p. 6. For similar explicit Syrian statements about annexing Lebanon, see Daniel Pipes, *Greater Syria: The History of an Ambition* (New York: Oxford University Press, 1990), pp. 119-21.

Syria's incentive to compromise or soften its negotiating position to reach a deal. This has in turn affected the pace of the negotiations, which have stalled every time Israel made progress (e.g., the Declaration of Principles and Arafat-Rabin handshake, the Cairo implementation agreement with the Palestinians, and the peace treaty with Jordan) on the other "tracks" of the peace process. Though other factors have contributed to Syria's tough stand and slow "pre-negotiations" with Israel,[4] consolidating its grip on Lebanon was certainly one of its more important considerations.

Many analysts have opined that Syria's first priority in the peace process is the survival and continuation of the regime, followed immediately by its control over Lebanon—in the minds of President Assad and the leadership in Damascus, the two are organically linked. Ensuring Syria's place in the Arab world (or securing Assad's name in Arab history) and improving political and economic relations with the United States are roughly third and fourth; retrieving the Golan Heights comes fifth.[5] Thus, the Syrians have been content to rely on the pressure generated on the Israelis by the precedent set in the Camp David accords, in which Israel agreed to return all of Sinai to Egypt in exchange for peace. The combination of the Sinai precedent and the "land for peace" formula that served as the basis for the Madrid conference has created momentum that promotes Syria's aim of the complete return of the Golan, and emboldened Syrian intransigence regarding any territorial concessions. The Syrians have expended little effort beyond recurrent rhetoric about full Israeli withdrawal from the Golan, and even less to clarify the nature of the ensuing peace once full withdrawal occurs. Since Netanyahu came to power in Israel and substituted "security" for "land" in the Madrid formula, Damascus has protested that willingness to return the Golan is a necessary condition for the resumption of negotiations and any resulting peace deal.

If Syria's honor and pride are invested in regaining the Golan Heights, its retention of control over Lebanon represents a vital (though rarely enunciated) interest related to the self-perceived well-being of the regime itself. After all, no matter how strategically or historically significant the barren Golan plateau may be to Syria, it cannot outweigh the acquisition—

---

[4] Among these are classic Syrian caution, Assad's proverbial patience, the nature of the Syrian regime, Syrian psychological inhibitions regarding full peace with Israel, the Likud government's priorities (including its reluctance to tax the Israeli public over the Golan Heights and other concessions to Syria), and Netanyahu's focus on security issues.

[5] Speech by Zalman Shoval, foreign policy advisor to Prime Minister Binyamin Netanyahu and former Israeli ambassador to the United States, at the Washington Institute for Near East Policy, May 11, 1995. Shoval listed Syria's priorities as 1) the survival and continuity of the regime, 2) retaining Lebanon, 3) its position in the Arab world and history, 4) relations with the United States, and 5) the return of the Golan. For similar readings of Syrian priorities, see Moshe Zak, "Syria's Game: Peres Versus Rabin," *Jerusalem Post*, November 24, 1995; Dore Gold, "Will the U.S. and Israel Sacrifice Lebanon for an Israeli-Syrian Peace?" *Moment* (April 1996), pp. 54-55; Avi-Ran, *Syrian Involvement in Lebanon Since 1975*, pp. 201-2; and Daniel Pipes, *Syria Beyond the Peace Process*, Policy Paper no. 40 (Washington, DC: Washington Institute, 1996).

even if partial—of an entire country, particularly when the appropriation also satisfies a deeply ingrained ideological atavism. When the issue of Lebanon is raised in the peace negotiations, the Syrian line is to insist on full Israeli withdrawal from the country while simultaneously emphasizing the intertwined nature (indeed, the "oneness") of the Lebanese and Syrian tracks. The Syrians also seem to be signaling that their continued paramount influence in Lebanon must go unquestioned during and especially after peace negotiations. For its part, Lebanon's "official" position in the negotiations (as permitted by Syria) does not extend beyond the incessant mantra of implementing United Nations Resolution 425, which calls for Israel's withdrawal from southern Lebanon. A corollary to this position is open support by the Lebanese government for the "resistance movements" engaged in liberating Israeli-occupied land in the south. This rigidly reductionist approach is the extent of the "peace" Syria is willing to allow Lebanon to "negotiate" with Israel.

Despite decades of bitter rancor, Israel and Syria have a pragmatic record of tacit security understandings in Lebanon dating back to the June-July 1976 "Red Line" agreement limiting the advance of Syrian forces entering war-ravaged Lebanon as the vanguard of an Arab deterrent force. Following the Syrian intervention, relations between the two drifted incrementally toward confrontation, culminating in a 1981 clash around the Christian city of Zahle in the Bekaa Valley. In response, the Syrians introduced Soviet-made surface-to-air missile (SAM) batteries in the Bekaa, in contravention of their understandings with Israel. Israel subsequently destroyed these SAMs at the outset of its 1982 invasion of Lebanon, and went on to destroy the PLO infrastructure in the country (which the Syrians did not mind too much) and weaken Syria's military posture there. The pre-war "red lines" were updated and modified to include a ban on Syrian military flights over Lebanon (in contrast to regular Israeli reconnaissance flights), a ban on Syrian SAMs in Lebanon or along Syria's western border with Lebanon, and the designation of the Awali River as the farthest point south—with the exception of the coastal city of Sidon—to which Syrian forces could advance.[6] Israel placed no limit, however, on the number of Syrian soldiers or civilians entering Lebanon.

---

[6] The best account to date of the complex Israeli-Syrian confrontations and *modus vivendi* in Lebanon remains Yair Evron, *War and Intervention in Lebanon: The Israeli-Syrian Deterrence Dialogue* (Baltimore: Johns Hopkins University Press, 1987); on the emergence, collapse, and reinstitution of the "Red Lines" agreement, see pp. 45-56, 63-64, 170-74; on the 1981-82 "missile crisis" and its brief recurrence in November 1985, see pp. 94-95, 135-37, 171-74, 193. Evron correctly emphasizes the important role an interested and influential third party such as the United States can play in a volatile arena of potential confrontation like Lebanon (pp. 88-90, 213-15). He concludes that the Israel-Syria "deterrence equation" is essentially rational and that the parties "did not search for victory, but rather for the management of military behavior" (p. 221). On the siege of Zahle and the missile crisis, see also Itamar Rabinovich, *The War for Lebanon, 1970-1985* (Ithaca, NY: Cornell University Press, 1985), pp. 118-20, and Ze'ev Schiff and Ehud Ya'ari, *Israel's Lebanon War*, ed. and trans. Ina Friedman, (New York: Simon & Schuster, 1984), pp. 31-35.

In October 1990, Israel and the United States tacitly acquiesced to the use of Syrian aircraft to oust Gen. Aoun from Lebanon's presidential palace. U.S. and Israeli tolerance of Syrian hegemony in Lebanon north of the security zone was motivated by the "fig leaf" of Arab nationalist support Syria provided for the anti-Iraq coalition in the Gulf, ill-timed overtures Aoun made to Saddam Hussein (as a counterbalance to Syria), and the mistaken belief that Damascus would control Islamist militants such as Hezbollah. Instead, these groups continued sporadically lobbing Katyusha rockets into northern Israel. This led to a cycle of retaliation that culminated in "Operation Accountability," a massive Israeli incursion in July 1993 designed to pressure the Lebanese government—and, by extension, the Syrians—to rein in Hezbollah by sending tens of thousands of civilians fleeing north toward Beirut.[7] The strategy worked and resulted in an informal, U.S.-brokered agreement between Israel and Hezbollah, which lasted for more than two years until the assassination of Islamic Jihad leader Fathi Shikaki in Malta in October 1995 initiated another round of reprisals and counterstrikes.

The agreement finally collapsed completely in April 1996, when Israel launched "Operation Grapes of Wrath," which included attacks on Lebanon's national infrastructure and Beirut itself, in response to renewed Hezbollah rocket attacks on northern Israel. The United States and France brokered a new arrangement known as "The Understanding" to end the fighting. The new agreement stipulated that armed groups in Lebanon would cease all attacks on Israel and the use of civilian areas and industrial installations to launch attacks on Israeli and allied forces in Lebanon; Israel would in turn refrain from targeting civilian areas in Lebanon; and nothing in the agreement would preclude any party from exercising the right of self-defense. In addition, the agreement established a monitoring group composed of the United States, France, Israel, Syria, and Lebanon to oversee the implementation of its provisions and review violations.[8]

Though replete with violations and breakdowns over the years, the official arrangements and undeclared mutual understandings between Syria and Israel in Lebanon demonstrate that the two sides are capable of interacting "prudently and rationally" in a desire to avoid unnecessary conflict in the Lebanese arena.[9] In theory, this bodes well for the Lebanon component of an Israel-Syria peace deal. Whether this will translate into a benevolent outcome for Lebanon (e.g., modest steps toward the restoration of Lebanese sovereignty and freedoms) is not certain and will probably depend to a considerable degree on the role the United States, the only credible and indispensable third party, decides to play during and, more pertinently, after the peace negotiations.

---

[7] David Makovsky, *Making Peace with the PLO* (Boulder, CO: Westview Press, 1996), pp. 91.
[8] For the text of the agreement in Arabic, see *al-Nahar*, April 27, 1996.
[9] Alasdair Drysdale and Raymond Hinnebusch, *Syria and the Middle East Peace Process* (New York: Council on Foreign Relations Press, 1991), p. 203.

Given Syria's overwhelming role in Lebanon since 1990, any understanding between Israel and the armed Islamists in the south is also an indirect understanding with the Syrians, who exercise substantial influence on these militant groups, principally Hezbollah. Conversely, any infringement of the understanding instigated by the Islamists must trigger speculation about a covert Syrian connection. In fact, Syrian links with Iran, the inspirer and financial backer of Hezbollah, are very close. They have ideological as well as strategic dimensions: the former having to do with an Alawi-Shi'a affinity and common fear of Sunni resurgence, and the latter entailing an anti-Iraq and anti-Israel alliance.[10] Syrian relations with Iran are not always smooth, however. They experienced some acrimony, for example, when Tehran exploited Israel's "Operation Grapes of Wrath" by attempting to strengthen its direct ties with Hezbollah, thereby bypassing Damascus. It was also revealed during the crisis that Iran had been organizing and funding a fundamentalist network inside Syria. The strains eventually subsided after some arrests and diplomatic posturing, but the episode is indicative of lingering mutual suspicions and incompatibilities between the two radical states.[11]

SYRIA'S REQUIREMENTS IN LEBANON

Syria and Israel both have a range of minimalist and maximalist interests and security requirements with respect to Lebanon that will need to be addressed in the context of any viable peace deal,[12] but in the short term Syria has the clear advantage. In theory, Syrian aims in Lebanon are limitless. Ba'th ideology regards Lebanon as an integral part of a "Greater Syria" and lost territory in the process of being recovered. According to the Ba'th claim, French and other historical Western encroachments breached and diluted Lebanon's "Arab identity," which needs to be restored and protected. This means that Lebanon's "purer" big brother to the east—the "throbbing heart of Arabism," as the popular saying goes—has the natural right to intervene in Lebanon, take charge of its affairs, rectify the historical wrong committed against it, and absorb it back into the Syrian-Arab fold where it belongs. (Ba'th ideology views Jordan, Iraq, historic Palestine, and the Turkish province of Hatay in a similar fashion; however, it is only in Lebanon that such expansionist ambitions can be fully

---

[10] For a discussion of the Syria-Iran relationship and its Lebanese dimensions, see Hussein J. Agha and Ahmad S. Khalidi, *Syria and Iran: Rivalry and Cooperation* (London: Pinter Publishers, 1995), pp. 3-7, 14-25, 77-82.

[11] See Tzaafa Hairi's dispatch from Paris on the tensions between Syria and Iran, published in *al-Watan al-'Arabi* (London), September, 27, 1996.

[12] For an overview of Syria's and Israel's interests in Lebanon, see Evron, *War and Intervention in Lebanon*, pp. 19-25 (Syria), 25-33 (Israel); see also Ze'ev Schiff, *Israel-Syria Negotiations: Lesson Learned, 1993–96*, Policy Paper no. 46 (Washington, DC: Washington Institute for Near East Policy, pending).

realized.) Therefore, to the ruling Ba'th party in Damascus it is ludicrous to equate the Israeli and Syrian presences in Lebanon under the heading "foreign occupations"—this designation certainly applies to Israel, but never to Syria, because Syria and Lebanon constitute one people in two states (in Ba'th terminology, *qutran* or "two statelets") that historically were one.[13] Thus, any call for the withdrawal of "foreign" forces from Lebanon does not concern Syria which, over the past twenty years, has amassed an impressive (though easily refutable) array of pseudo-legal justifications for its entry into Lebanon.[14]

Although Syrian Ba'th irredentism in relation to Lebanon is contrived and rests on no firm historical basis,[15] it is hardly the sole motivation for Syria's interest in its western neighbor. Beyond ideology, there are

---

[13] For an account of Ba'th ideology and the relationship between pan-Syrianism (i.e, "Greater Syria") and pan-Arabism, see Daniel Pipes, *Greater Syria*, pp. 37-38, 43, 45-51, 155-58. On the Syrian view of the difference between their presence in Lebanon and Israel's, see Patrick Seale, *Asad of Syria: The Struggle for the Middle East* (Berkeley, CA: University of California Press, 1989), p. 413. Seale quotes Syrian President Assad as telling U.S. envoy Robert McFarlane in June 1983 that "Syria's influence was legitimate and had to prevail [because] Syria and Lebanon were one people, one nation, one geography [but] Israel was an alien presence." Seale also quotes from an Assad interview in the *Los Angeles Times* (August 14, 1983) in which he reiterates the same view. In his book *Battling For Peace: A Memoir* (New York: Random House, 1995), p. 194, Shimon Peres reveals a letter from Assad to Fidel Castro, intercepted by Israeli intelligence, in which Assad explains that the purpose of his intervention in Lebanon is to prevent the creation of a Christian state there.

[14] The "invitation" to enter Lebanon in 1976 that Syria always cites was actually formally revoked by Presidents Sarkis (1982) and Gemayel (1983) and by Prime Minister Aoun (1989). The argument that the Taif accord relegitimized the Syrian military and political presence in Lebanon begs the question, since a sizable and credible internal and external Lebanese opposition rejects the view that Taif can confer such legal authority.

[15] In a non-ideological context, "Greater Syria" (or *Bilad ash-Sham*) was always a geographic appellation similar to "North America," not a political designation. In *Greater Syria*, Daniel Pipes writes that "ecology and culture (but not politics) give historic Syria some cohesion" (p. 15) and "[t]hough universally recognized for more than two thousand years as a cohesive region, Syria is not a polity" (p. 16). If anything, he adds, "Mount Lebanon is the region of Greater Syria with the longest tradition as a political entity" (p. 33). Furthermore, a political party coming to power through a *coup d'etat* can hardly legitimately claim to represent or speak on behalf of a presumed political entity from the past. The Ba'th will therefore have a hard time making a convincing case that they are the true heirs to a historical Syria that included Lebanon, because none ever existed.

They are on even shakier ground pretending to harbor a grievance about France's 1920 creation of Greater Lebanon, because no territory was taken away from any clearly defined and internationally recognized independent political entity called Syria. Before the French Mandate, the area in question was part of the Ottoman Empire and organized according to the wishes and needs of the sultan in Istanbul. If anything, Lebanon—Mount Lebanon, to be specific—has a sound historical basis for making claims of distinctive political and cultural apartness. Historian Meir Zamir writes that "[t]he history of Lebanon as a separate entity began neither in 1920 with the creation of the modern state nor in 1861 with the establishment of the autonomous Sanjak of Mount Lebanon (the Mutasarrifiya). In fact, it is doubtful whether any other country in the Middle East apart from Egypt can claim such a long, continuous history as a political entity. Certain unique features had already appeared as far back as the Mamluke period"; see Zamir, *The Formation of Modern Lebanon*, pp. 4-5.

concrete security considerations that drive Syrian activities in Lebanon. The regime has always linked its own survival to its control over events in Lebanon, including political control in Beirut. There is some justification for this view, because many of the coups in pre-Assad Syria were engineered in Beirut. For this reason, Syria always sought to have a hand in the formation of various Lebanese governments and to influence Lebanese presidential elections. Moreover, Syria's domestic political balance often extends to a number of Lebanese families and factions, so that unrest in one place is invariably reflected in the other.[16] Damascus therefore feels the need for constant vigilance, lest a group or combination of factions hostile to Syria takes over in Lebanon.

Lebanese society has always been more free and open than Syrian society, so it was only natural that the winds of change should blow east from the Mediterranean coast and high mountains and not the other way around. Over the past twenty years, however, Syria's highly intrusive response to security challenges in Lebanon has been completely disproportionate to their actual magnitude. In classic totalitarian fashion, Damascus' response has been to attempt in a variety of ways to stifle Lebanon's climate of freedom in the name of "security." Maximally defined, Syria's security imperatives in Lebanon amount to total control of the country, an aim that it is methodically pursuing.

Syria's security requirements in Lebanon *vis-à-vis* Israel center on two main considerations. First, the Bekaa Valley must be either under its direct control or within easy access of its military forces, or that it be neutralized with ironclad international guarantees (that only the United States could provide) to prevent a possible Israeli land attack. Related to this is Syria's insistence on Israeli evacuation of southern Lebanon. Second, Syria strives to deprive Israel of any actual or potential allies among the various Lebanese communities. It has been largely successful in its efforts since the mid-1980s to dismantle Israeli-Christian cooperation and neutralize the Israeli-Druze connection in Lebanon.

In addition, Syria's predominant position in Lebanon offers enormous economic and political opportunities there. The country has become a veritable playground for the Syrian ruling class. Not only are senior members of the Syrian government and military making windfall profits in a variety of ways in Lebanon, at any given point in time there are several hundred thousand Syrian workers in Lebanon who constitute a large and cheap labor force that is displacing Lebanese workers. Lebanon also serves as a convenient dumping ground for potential troublemakers in Syria, who

---

[16] Patrick Seale sums it up neatly when he writes that "the political temperature of the one could not but affect that of the other"; see Seale, *Asad of Syria*, p. 269. For a discussion of the domestic considerations that have motivated Syria's involvement in Lebanon—such as avoiding conflicts of interest at home, appeasing rivals within the ruling coalition in Damascus, and bolstering financial and material resources by tapping into Lebanon's rich offerings, see Fred H. Lawson, *Why Syria Goes to War: Thirty Years of Confrontation* (Ithaca, NY: Cornell University Press, 1996), pp. 76-97.

are sent across the border either as workers or as regular soldiers. Through its influence in Lebanon, particularly an extensive and largely unseen intelligence apparatus, Syria can monitor and curb radical groups such as Hezbollah, as well as any resurgence of Palestinian activity. Lebanon thus provides Damascus with so-called "plausible deniability" that allows it to avoid accountability for the actions it undertakes there and elsewhere by proxy.[17]

Syria's continued control over key ministries in the Lebanese government—foreign affairs, defense, interior, and labor—is vital for maintaining its political influence and safeguarding its security interests there. The remaining portfolios can to some degree be subject to the vicissitudes of internal Lebanese factional politics; these four crucial posts, however, are not negotiable and must be headed by sycophants securely in Damascus' control. Once Lebanon's free-wheeling media has been effectively castrated and silenced, a fifth cabinet post (minister of information) can be added to the list of the four "untouchables."

In its attempts to consolidate its control over Lebanon, Syria has sought to move beyond mere operatives and puppets and acquire credible partners who would legitimize its presence there. As the Christians have been most opposed to Syrian predations, they would presumably make the best candidates for such an endeavor. So far, however, Syria's feeble overtures to some Christian leaders have been spurned, with the exception of the Franjieh clan, which has strong ties to the Assad family predating the Lebanon war, and some already discredited political figures in the Christian community. The Maronite patriarch, for example, was the object of several indirect Syrian entreaties, yet his Sunday sermons remained outspokenly critical of the policies and human rights violations of the Lebanese authorities and by implication the Syrians.[18]

The linchpin of Syria's indefinite stay in Lebanon is its self-appointed and carefully cultivated security role in the country. With the Lebanese army and internal security forces weakened, in the eyes of the outside

---

[17] The examples are too numerous to list. Most glaring is the continuous mayhem in southern Lebanon, in contrast with years of absolute quiet on the Golan—Syria is more or less equally in charge in both places. The Syrians similarly allowed Hezbollah supporters to pour into the streets of Beirut and celebrate Rabin's assassination, while the streets of Damascus remained quiet and Syrian radio reported the event without comment. Finally, pro-Syrian officials and media in Lebanon frequently use the term "Zionist enemy" even as most of the rest of the Arabs—including Syria—now refer to Israel by name; in the 1960s and 1970s, the situation was reversed.

[18] For examples of the patriarch's remarks during the first half of 1995, in which he was critical of specific government policies, the stifling political climate, arbitrary imprisonment, torture, deteriorating economic conditions, an unfair judicial system, and Christian emigration, see *al-Diyar*, February 28, 1995; *al-Nahar*, March 20, 1995; *al-Nahar*, April 15, 1995; *al-Nahar*, April 18, 1995; *al-Nahar*, April 22, 1995; *al-Diyar*, May 4, 1995; *al-Safir*, May 5, 1995; and *al-Anwar*, May 14, 1995. Throughout the summer of 1996, the patriarch spoke out repeatedly against the irregularities plaguing both the preparations for and the conduct of the Syrian-managed Lebanese parliamentary elections.

world the massive Syrian military and security presence in Lebanon has been the only guarantee against a resumption of fighting among the various Lebanese factions. During the years of war in Lebanon, Syria at one time or another both championed and fought against every faction and group in the country, sometimes supplying arms and on other occasions threatening to discontinue the supplies. As the situation in Lebanon settled to a slow boil, Syria gradually insinuated and entrenched itself in the ravaged country. In its new capacity as peacekeeper in Lebanon, Syria resembles a pyromaniac turned firefighter.[19] The international community often conveniently overlooks the dual role that Damascus has perfected.

Syria simply has too much invested in Lebanon to relinquish or diminish its control easily.[20] Due to Syria's vast destabilizing and retaliatory potential in Lebanon—and the fact that physically dislodging it would be too costly—the alternative that has gradually emerged has been grudging acknowledgment by both Israel and the United States of Syria's "pacifying" and "security" roles there. This sense of resignation is also prevalent among Lebanon's internal actors—after twenty years of vicious internecine conflict, a hesitant but genuine communal consensus has emerged in favor of some form of peaceful coexistence and against a return to sectarian strife.

Thus, the cynical and oft-repeated statement that if the Syrians withdrew in the morning, the Lebanese would be at each other's throats by noon—which might have applied three or four years ago—is no longer valid. In addition to general war-weariness on all sides, the Lebanese penchant for political compromise, and the lure of the economic benefits of coexistence, specific external causes of previous unrest are either absent or on the wane: the Palestinian factor—a key ignitor of the Lebanon war in 1975—is missing, and there is a dawning realization among Iran's Lebanese clients that the Islamic Republic's artificial and transitory influence in the eastern Mediterranean has peaked and is ebbing. If unduly pressured, Syria could instigate factional unrest in Lebanon to reassert the importance of its security role. But a return to full-scale hostilities and civil war is unlikely, and such Syrian instigations would be recognized for what they are.

Damascus remains very jealous about its self-defined regional role and importance. In fact, the phrase "Syria's regional role" has become a euphemism for, among other things, Syria's domination of Lebanon, which has emerged as the centerpiece of its regional self-image.[21] This

---

[19] Interview with Michel Aoun in *Middle East Quarterly* 2, no. 4 (December 1995), p. 59.
[20] Drysdale and Hinnebusch, *Syria and the Middle East Peace Process*, p. 128.
[21] "More important for us than recovering the Golan is Syria's regional role, and this is a main negotiating point," declared an unnamed high-level Syrian official in *al-Sharq al-Awsat*, December 14, 1995. Although the statement was made in the context of Syrian concerns over the fate of Iraq, the article discloses a Syrian proposal to create a "Fertile Crescent" partnership among Iraq, Syria, and Lebanon. Syria's control over Lebanon is clearly viewed as a springboard for its larger "regional role."

issue is not open for dispute in negotiations with Israel. The legitimization of its hegemony in Lebanon is one of Syria's minimum demands in an eventual peace deal with Israel and—along with full Israeli withdrawal from the Golan—is very close to its *maximum* requirements. The only difference between the former and the latter is the degree of eventual Syrian control over Lebanon. It may be to Damascus' advantage to maintain the diplomatic fiction of an independent Lebanon and reap the benefits of its ostensible statehood (such as a seat in the United Nations)— as the Soviets did with Belarus and the Ukraine—rather than insisting on a complete merger or outright annexation. Syria's ruling Alawi minority might also wish to avoid its further demographic dilution that total absorption would precipitate. In this sense, a "virtual" Lebanon constitutes a convenient safety valve.

There are real fears in Lebanon about a number of scenarios that involve the culmination of its imperceptible but ongoing ingestion by Syria. These scenarios share one or more of the following elements: more imposed bilateral agreements, some kind of economic or even political confederation between Syria and Lebanon, and use of the new parliament resulting from the carefully staged 1996 elections to further consolidate and legitimize Syria's grip on Lebanon in every way short of blatant annexation. These parliamentary measures could include the elimination of the confessional system that has served as the basis of Lebanese politics since independence, legislation of further mass naturalizations (mostly of Syrian Muslims) that would create a demographic *fait accompli*, continued indifference to the growing number of human rights violations perpetrated by the Beirut government, a sustained assault on Lebanon's liberal educational sector, and steps toward Islamicization (similar to those in other Arab states) such as declaring Friday an end-of-the-week holiday.

A view prevalent in certain circles in Washington and Jerusalem is that President Assad somehow "missed his chance" by not signing a peace treaty with Israel when first Yitzhak Rabin and then Shimon Peres offered him what seemed like favorable terms, particularly compared to the reversals and retractions under Netanyahu.[22] In fact, the Syrian leader heaved a figurative sigh of relief—audible in Beirut—when the peace momentum generated by Peres' policies ground to a halt with the May 1996 Likud victory. He did indeed miss his chance—*by design*.[23] The prospect of full and real peace, followed by swift normalization with Israel, had always represented a tremendous risk for the cautious Assad, and he had a

---

[22] David Makovsky labeled Assad "the Great Miscalculator"; see *Jerusalem Post*, June 15, 1996. Kenneth M. Pollack, on the other hand, argues that Assad is "caught on the horns of a dilemma" between keeping Lebanon by forfeiting peace, and jeopardizing his hold over Lebanon by embracing a peace deal; see Pollack, "Peace and the Syrian Dilemma," *PeaceWatch* no. 109, Washington Institute for Near East Policy (October 28, 1996).

[23] Some commentators actually made this point rather forcefully; see Thomas L. Friedman, "Israel's Arab Fallout," *New York Times*, June 5, 1996; and Charles Krauthammer, "Clinton to Assad: The Letter He Never Sent," *Washington Post*, June 7, 1996.

decided preference for the peace process over peace itself. Syria's self-sustained status as the principal confrontation Arab state and useful Iranian connections simply could not survive such a peace—at least not before Assad secures his succession and absorbs Lebanon to the point of irreversibility. An open-ended, "no peace, no war" status quo therefore remains Assad's best option and, obversely, Lebanon's worst-case scenario.

Contrary to the September 1996 "war scare" hype in the Israeli press (brought on by sudden Syrian troop movements in Lebanon that month), Assad was not preparing to launch a surprise attack. Throughout the summer, the Syrians had been genuinely apprehensive about threats both oblique and direct from the new Likud government that Hezbollah's next violation of "The Understanding" would invite retaliation aimed at Syrian forces stationed inside Lebanon.[24] Israel's July 2 airstrikes against Palestinian positions in the eastern Bekaa three miles from the Syrian border (and only 200 yards from the headquarters of Ghazi Kanaan, Syria's intelligence chief in Lebanon), underscored the seriousness of Netanyahu's implied threats.[25]

Looking exclusively at Syria's actions in Lebanon in order to assess its overall posture can yield a deceptive picture. Though reasonably secure about their control of Lebanon, the Syrians have plenty to worry about on the regional level, which could easily reflect back adversely on Syria's position there. The February 1996 announcement, for example, of an Israel-Turkey military cooperation agreement profoundly rattled the Syrian leadership. Reports circulating in April 1996 that Israeli warplanes were based and training in Turkey only served to increase Syrian nervousness during Israel's "Operation Grapes of Wrath" in Lebanon. These reports coincided with strong anti-Syrian statements by the Turkish government, which was angered by Syria's continued support for the Kurdish Workers Party (PKK). Suddenly, the prospect of a two-front war loomed in the distance.

The resulting panic in Damascus was reflected in an immediate and massive call-up of thousands of Syrian army conscripts and reserves doubling as construction workers, vegetable vendors, and other laborers in Lebanon. Their swift exodus at the time was noticed and reported by many in Lebanon. Although most eventually returned when the tension settled, the incident not only revealed a precarious aspect of Syria's presence in

---

[24] On June 11, 1996, Netanyahu issued threats against Hezbollah and, by implication, Syria following the ambush of Israeli soldiers in southern Lebanon; see *Washington Times*, June 12, 1996. Some newspaper editorials had already been urging an Israeli retaliatory strike against Syrian forces in Lebanon or Syria itself; see George Melloan, "Playing Mouse to Hafez Assad's Cat," and Albert Wohlstetter, "A Perilous 'Partnership for Peace'," *Wall Street Journal*, May 6 and 22, 1996, respectively. Following the stillborn "Lebanon First" proposal, Netanyahu warned that an "escalation of violence in Lebanon is not something that is good for Syria and . . . Israel"; see *Washington Post*, August 6, 1996. For assessments of the Israeli government's threats against the Syrians in Lebanon, see also the articles by Ze'ev Schiff in *Ha'aretz*, June 14, July 5, August 16, and August 30, 1996.

[25] See *New York Times* and *Washington Times*, July 3, 1996.

Lebanon, but also emphasized a widely known fact—namely, that Syria cannot realistically face an external foe such as Turkey or Israel (much less both) and hope to win. Syria's armed forces are only effective in controlling the Syrian and Lebanese people, and keeping the Damascus regime in power.

ISRAEL'S REQUIREMENTS IN LEBANON

Israel's maximal requirements in Lebanon in theory include full normalization and all the benefits deriving from a warm peace. Since Israel's bitter 1982-83 invasion of Lebanon, there has been a steady drift toward the absolute minimum: security arrangements negotiated with Syria and ultimately guaranteed by the United States.

The idea of a natural solidarity among the non-Muslim minorities in the Middle East is an old one. Earlier this century, there were tenuous Maronite-Zionist overtures. Maronite Archbishop Ignatius Mubarak and Maronite Patriarch Antoine Arida, for example, participated in faltering attempts to establish contacts between Maronite and Zionist leaders at the end of World War I, but nothing came of these efforts because neither side was sure of the other's intentions.[26] After the establishment of the state of Israel, the internal debate among Israeli leaders about a strategy toward Lebanon's Christians (and particularly the Maronites) revealed a tendency to seek operatives rather than true partners or allies.[27]

The concept of an Israeli-Christian entente was revived following the outbreak of the Lebanon war in 1975, and received added impetus after the Syrians entered Lebanon in 1976 and later turned against the Christians. The uneasy relationship between the two non-Muslim minorities reached a crescendo with Israel's 1982 invasion of Lebanon, and then—plagued from the outset by an infernal combination of misperceptions and flaws in the outlooks, expectations, and actions of both parties—unraveled terribly.[28] The successive fiascoes of Bashir Gemayel's assassination, the Sabra and Shatila massacres, and Israel's stillborn May 1983 agreement with Lebanon were the relationship's *coups de grace*. The

---

[26] For an in-depth discussion of early Maronite-Zionist encounters, see Laura Zittrain Eisenberg, *My Enemy's Enemy: Lebanon in the Early Zionist Imagination, 1900-1948* (Detroit, MI: Wayne State University Press, 1994).

[27] On Moshe Sharett's exchange with David Ben-Gurion and Moshe Dayan about " 'buy[ing]' a Maronite officer who would then 'invite' Israeli intervention in Lebanese affairs and enable Israel to establish its control over Lebanon," see Schiff and Ya'ari, *Israel's Lebanon War*, pp. 13-14.

[28] To date, there has been no comprehensive scholarly analysis of the tortured relationship between Israeli Jews and Lebanese Christians, despite a growing body of literature on the aftermath of the phase of the Lebanon war initiated by Israel's 1982 invasion. Analysis that manages to go beyond a litany of recriminations usually suffers from an excess of polemics and partisanship, understandably conditioned by the lingering trauma of those events. The time has come for this tragic topic and all its ramifications to be responsibly revisited.

ill-conceived alliance was quickly replaced by a loss of confidence, mutual bitterness, and increasingly cynical caution. Israel exchanged its exclusive bilateral relationship with Lebanon's Christians in favor of pragmatic deals with a variety of communities in Lebanon, mainly the Druze and the Shi'a. On more than one occasion, Israel's coordinator of activities in Lebanon, Uri Lubrani, made its policy shift clear to querying Christians.

Though it seemed to work for a while, the new policy eventually revealed its inherent limitations, and Israel ultimately concluded that dealing with strong states in the region—even authoritarian regimes that maintain stability by ruling with an "iron fist"—was preferable to unpredictable sub-state actors. In Lebanon's case, this meant Syria. As early as 1982, while the invasion of Lebanon was still underway, Israeli officials from both Labor and Likud made impromptu visits to the homes of Lebanese Christians. During one, then-Labor opposition leader Yitzhak Rabin said in no uncertain terms that a shift was coming in Israeli policy in favor of making a deal with Syria, and urged the Lebanese—and particularly the Christians—to achieve a *modus vivendi* with the Syrians.[29] In a 1984 meeting with Christian militia leaders in Tel Aviv, Rabin repeated the same point and concluded with the words, "pragma, not dogma," which were promptly transmitted back to and circulated around Lebanon.

Rabin's advice accurately reflected the new direction Israeli priorities were taking at the time, but underestimated the growing chasm between Syria's ruthlessly implemented expansionist intentions and the tenacious authenticity of Lebanese patriotic resistance. Accommodation with the Syrians did subsequently occur, but soon met with severe and inevitable limitations: In matters pertaining to a people's ultimate destiny and residing in the deepest recesses of their being, fundamental principles and values—"dogma"—cannot be persistently and exhaustively sacrificed at the altar of "pragma." The result was renewed polarization and confrontation.

The allergic reaction that Israeli politicians—and, more importantly, the Israeli public—developed to anything related to Lebanon in the wake of the 1982 invasion has precluded any serious policy of engagement in Lebanon's problems *north* of the security zone. After 1983, Israel reverted to a policy of reaction in Lebanon, with the aim of avoiding the Lebanese morass.[30] At a 1992 U.S. Institute of Peace forum in Washington, Professor Itamar Rabinovich (who later served as Israel's ambassador to the United States) explained that no Israeli government then or in the foreseeable future could devise a policy of active involvement north of the security zone and expect to secure Knesset endorsement or popular support for it.

---

[29] The author vividly recalls Rabin's sudden appearance (with a few associates) at his home on a suburban hill overlooking Beirut.

[30] Evron, *War and Intervention in Lebanon*, p. 32. In 1976 Rabin, Peres, and then Chief-of-Staff Mordechai Gur all made statements to the effect that a Syrian takeover of Lebanon would be a grave security threat to Israel—despite their cautious, "rational" avoidance of the developing Lebanese quagmire; see pp. 36-39.

Israel's first priority in Lebanon is to guarantee the security of its northern border, including the towns and settlements of the northern Galilee. This means a complete and permanent cessation of all cross-border attacks by Hezbollah or any other armed group, and the prevention of the return to the area of rejectionist Palestinian organizations opposed to the peace process. This would most likely entail reaching an agreement with Syria, Israel's interlocutor on security in Lebanon, under which Damascus would allow the Lebanese army to deploy into the security zone (perhaps all the way to the international border) to disarm the militias and re-assert Lebanese authority there.

Second, Israel would require that such an agreement ensure that the Bekaa Valley does not remain a breeding and training ground for militant pro-Iranian paramilitaries and other terrorist groups, that Syria reduce and restructure its own military presence there to a purely defensive posture, and that it not extend south of the town of Mashghara. The details of actual deployments, buffer zones, international observers or peacekeeping forces, early warning systems, verification regimes, *et cetera* would be worked out in negotiations, and implementation of the agreement would be guaranteed by the United States.

Third, Israel would insist that the South Lebanon Army (SLA), a proxy force of about 2,500[31] mostly Christian and Shi'a men from southern Lebanon, be absorbed and integrated into the existing Lebanese army, and that serious efforts be made to prevent a cycle of vendettas and reprisals from erupting. Once a satisfactory agreement is reached, Israel would no longer need a "security zone" in southern Lebanon, where its soldiers have been sustaining casualties in a war of slow attrition, and would withdraw completely from Lebanon.

Hezbollah has already given oblique indications that it is beginning to prepare for a post-peace process political role in Lebanon.[32] Syria's willingness and ability to enforce some of the other aspects of a peace agreement in Lebanon—such as containing reprisals against members of the SLA, allowing the Lebanese army to assume responsibility for security duties, redeploying its forces from the Beirut area to the Bekaa as required

---

[31] "Last Front of Arab-Israeli Warfare: Lebanon," *New York Times*, December 18, 1995.

[32] In an interview with *Die Zeit* (December 20, 1994), Hezbollah Secretary-General Sheikh Hassan Nasrallah said that resistance to Israel would end with the signing of an Israel-Syria peace agreement. This change in Hezbollah's policy orientation was further demonstrated by its participation in the 1992 and 1996 Lebanese parliamentary elections, in which several of their candidates were elected on both occasions. Hezbollah broadcasts constantly refer to the peace process as the *taswiya* (settlement), suggesting a recognition that a new situation is unfolding. (However, the choice of *taswiya* also indicates that the organization regards the approaching peace as essentially provisional.) In addition, prominent Shi'a clerics sympathetic to Hezbollah's anti-Israeli activities have consistently called for the liberation of the south from Israeli occupation, but added that they merely oppose normalization with Israel after the "settlement." Sheikh Mohammad Mahdi Shamseddine, for example, spiritual leader of the Shi'a Higher Council in Lebanon, aired these views during a private trip to the United States in December 1995.

under the Taif agreement (or withdrawing completely from Lebanon, as called for in UN Resolution 520), closing terrorist training bases in the Bekaa (including those of the Kurdish PKK), and curtailing its close relationship with Iran in Lebanon—remain open questions.

These issues may not be as central to Israel's efforts to reach a peace deal with Syria as they are for Lebanon. Israeli policymakers and military officials maintain a deep-seated skepticism of Lebanon's ability to ensure its own security and stability, much less to assume sole responsibility for maintaining the security of Israel's northern border by quelling any potential threat that might originate from Lebanese territory. From their point of view, Syria—if it can be enticed to do so as part of a peace settlement without unacceptable concessions—is the better choice. This suits the Syrians, who have no intention of embarking on any step that might risk their continued usefulness or hegemony in Lebanon.

Dangling Lebanon as a convenient means of luring the Syrians into a peace deal appears to be the common denominator in the negotiation strategies of both Labor and Likud. On several occasions before and during their preliminary negotiations with Syria, Israeli officials of both the Labor and Likud parties floated the idea of offering *de facto* recognition of Syria's presence in Lebanon in return for a Syrian guarantee to end cross-border attacks on Israel and stabilize southern Lebanon.[33] The most recent version of this recurring idea was the Netanyahu government's "Lebanon First" proposal in August 1996, which envisioned Israel's withdrawal from the security zone in return for Syria's dismantling of Hezbollah's military wing, deployment of the Lebanese army to the border with Israel, and guarantees for the safety of the SLA.[34] Fearing loss of leverage over the return of the Golan Heights and the anticipated pressures to withdraw its forces from Lebanon after Israel pulled out, Damascus signaled the

---

[33] By not objecting to Syria's emphatic veto of the idea of a separate Israeli peace with Lebanon in August 1994, the late Yitzhak Rabin, for example, appeared to follow the lead of U.S. Secretary of State Warren Christopher and endorse Syria's permanent control over Lebanon; see "Assad Would Accept Peace, But He Lacks Trust," *Washington Times*, August 17, 1994 (originally in *London Observer*); see also Joseph Fitchett, "Rabin Indicates Acceptance of Syrian Authority in Lebanon," *International Herald Tribune*, August 24, 1994. In an interview with the Danish newspaper *Politiken* (February 13, 1995), Hebrew University historian and Syria expert Moshe Ma'oz declared that "Israel expects or requests that the Syrians rule in Lebanon notwithstanding the loss of Lebanon's sovereignty. The Lebanese are unable to rule themselves."

In an April 18, 1995 interview in *Ha'aretz*, then-Foreign Minister Shimon Peres stated that an Israel-Syria agreement would recognize Syria's "special status" in Lebanon. "Whether or not we say so in public," he added, "we realize one negotiation is being held on two countries." In the *Ha'aretz* weekly magazine (April 25, 1995), Peres laid out the contours of a deal with Syria that would give Assad both Lebanon and the Golan in return for peace. In an interview broadcast on Israel radio (April 19, 1600 GMT) and appearing in *Ma'ariv*, then-Deputy Foreign Minister Yossi Beilin repeated Peres' "offer" by saying that if a peace agreement were signed with Syria, it would not be important who is in control of southern Lebanon as long as the safety of Israel's northern residents were guaranteed.

[34] On "Lebanon First," see *Jerusalem Post*, August 9, 1996.

Lebanese authorities to reject the Israeli proposal and instead repeat their insistence on unconditional Israeli withdrawal as demanded by UN Resolution 425 of 1978.[35]

The "Lebanon First" offer confirmed for the Syrians that Israel was indeed suffering from the continuous trickle of casualties in southern Lebanon, due mainly to Hezbollah's newly acquired sophistication in low-intensity warfare. This reinforced President Assad's determination to continue applying pressure on Israel by rejecting the offer. Assad had become convinced that Netanyahu was doing his utmost to hold on to the Golan indefinitely. Accepting a deal on Lebanon, Assad reasoned, would have eroded Syria's negotiating position on the Golan and could well have endangered his greater prize, Lebanon.

Washington and Jerusalem's tacit approval of Syria's *de facto* dominion over Lebanon implies a willingness to recognize—and thus legitimize—it as part of a formal peace agreement.[36] This kind of *de jure* recognition by the international community would supersede Taif, thereby relieving Syria of any obligation to redeploy in or withdraw from Lebanon in the future. In the absence of strict conditions, formal recognition of Syria's preponderance in Lebanon could pave the way for an influx of Syrian troops into the country with the stated mission of preserving security and stability. Damascus has already used the pretext of reconstruction to send hundreds of thousands of "laborers" across the border. A peace deal leading to *de jure* acceptance of Syrian hegemony in Lebanon would amount to the final nail in the coffin of Lebanese sovereignty.

This is hardly the only option. The Lebanese "carrot" could be turned into a "stick": Syria's occupation could be made a source of mounting "costs" if it refuses to strike a satisfactory deal with Israel. Indeed, there has been a sporadic debate in Israel's political and military circles about the costs and benefits of a prolonged Syrian occupation of Lebanon. Militarily, Syria reduces its offensive capability and readiness by spreading its forces between the Golan and the Bekaa.[37] Politically, it risks incurring the wrath of the Lebanese population while its soldiers and officers contract Lebanon's "virus" of corruption and unregulated "back room" dealing that weakens Syria's overall military and political posture. At the same time, Syria is expanding its sphere of influence in Lebanon, consolidating its hold on the country's various resources (financial, natural, human, *et cetera*), and could emerge stronger in the long run.

---

[35] See "Hot October in Lebanon," *Foreign Report*, August 22, 1996 (Brighton, UK: Jane's Information Group, Ltd.).

[36] Tacit U.S. and Israeli acceptance of Syrian domination over Lebanon goes back at least to Syria's support for the anti-Iraq Gulf War coalition. For an analysis of how Lebanon is being used to lure the Syrians into a peace deal with Israel, see "Mideast Prize: Syria Tightens Its Grip on Lebanon, May Get Indefinite Control of It," *Wall Street Journal*, July 19, 1995.

[37] See Michael Eisenstadt, *Arming For Peace? Syria's Elusive Quest For "Strategic Parity*," Policy Paper no. 31 (Washington, DC: Washington Institute for Near East Policy, 1992), pp. 57-58. See also Shimon Peres, *Battling For Peace: A Memoir*, p. 199.

As the precarious Israel-Syria negotiations evolved, it became evident that Lebanon was not being used as a carrot *or* a stick—it had sunk to the status of a commodity that was Syria's "price" or "prize" for participating. History instructs that whenever two states with different political systems based on divergent (if not opposing) values negotiate, early appeasement of the less democratic state invariably complicates the bargaining process and does not yield the desired result of a satisfactory deal. Stalling and hardening negotiating positions become convenient means for the appeased state to gain additional time to absorb and consolidate its grip on the concessions received without having to reciprocate. Churchill tried in vain to convey this to Roosevelt in 1945 regarding the consequences of conceding Soviet control over Eastern Europe.

Considering Israeli policy since 1983, the argument favoring Syria's unconditional seizure of Lebanon is clearly ascendant. Given that neither a full and durable Israel-Syria peace nor an Israel-Syria military confrontation seems imminent, Israel appears willing to sacrifice Lebanese independence and sovereignty in a partial peace or an indefinite perpetuation of the status quo. Since the election of Binyamin Netanyahu, the latter appears to be the preferred option for both Jerusalem and Damascus. The Likud government opposes a "land for peace" formula *vis-à-vis* Syria and the Golan Heights; conversely, the Ba'thist regime has been breathing easier since the "threat" of imminent peace subsided and it gained a respite to consolidate its control over Lebanon. An intensification of Hezbollah's attrition campaign against Israeli forces in southern Lebanon could alter the status quo, but as long as Syria keeps the level of Israel's losses at a tolerable threshold, it can forestall or avert adverse changes in the power configuration on the ground.

Continued stagnation in the peace process is Lebanon's worst-case scenario. The amount of time that would be required to restart the Israeli-Syrian peace negotiations and then make progress at the previous glacial pace bodes ill for Lebanon's future prospects. Assuming that the peace process resumes, however, there is a vast difference from Lebanon's perspective between a "successful" outcome that serves Lebanon's interests and one that comes at Lebanon's expense. For Lebanon, the only test of the success or failure of the peace process is the extent to which it helps to restore the country's usurped sovereignty and liberate its besieged freedoms. As Israel commenced negotiations with Syria after Madrid, voices from both the Labor and Likud parties essentially conceded Lebanon. Labor "doves," feeling the pressure to clinch an agreement with Syria before elections in May 1996, were ready to give up both Lebanon and the Golan in return for security and full peace. Labor would have swallowed even a truncated peace—the only kind Assad has been willing to offer—for the sake of attaining a comprehensive agreement.

By contrast, the Likud government did not press the Syrians for full peace with normalization, but instead signaled in essence that Damascus could keep Lebanon, Jerusalem would keep the Golan, and both sides would be satisfied with a partial peace. From Assad's point of view, the Labor offer was more attractive—provided it didn't press for total peace with normalization—especially when the added sweetener of Syria's inflated regional role, as repeatedly depicted by Peres, was factored in.[38] The accelerating momentum toward full peace under Peres scared the reticent Assad, however. Under Netanyahu, a more familiar script is being played out: caution, tough talk, no impending deals, and more of the old hostility on which the Damascus regime has thrived. In such an atmosphere, Lebanon stays with Syria, meaning Syria stays in Lebanon, for the foreseeable future.

LOST OPPORTUNITY

Real peace is designed to bolster civil societies, not regimes. There has been much speculation about the likely "temperature" of a comprehensive peace in the Middle East. In thermal terms, when peace between Israel and the Arab states finally prevails, it will generally be two-tiered: a thick and pervasive "cool" peace beneath a much thinner "tepid" layer containing some distinctly "warm" spots throughout the region. The degree of warmth will be determined primarily by the respective natures of the societies involved, although the structures of the governments themselves can either impede or accelerate the process of opening up to, and creatively interacting with, the other.

By its very nature, Lebanon's society renders its people prime candidates for warm relations under a full and durable peace. Despite calls from some quarters in Lebanon for a continued boycott of Israel even after peace comes, and feverish mobilization by certain groups against the prospect of impending normalization, normalization will be unstoppable once it begins. Household-to-household interaction—which has largely eluded the Israel-Egypt relationship—could occur on a wide scale fairly swiftly in the case of Lebanon and soon pick up pace with the Palestinians and Jordanians. For normalization to attain unprecedented levels, however, Lebanon and Syria have to be sufficiently decoupled. Otherwise, opportunities in the economic and social spheres such as joint tourist enterprises, commercial projects, water resource management, academic and cultural exchanges, and a host of related activities, if they take place at all, will remain very modest in scope and constrained in their reach. Lebanon will be artificially confined to the cool tier of Mideast peace, which is the maximum Assad's Syria can tolerate.

---

[38] On Peres' view of the pivotal position Syria occupies in the Middle East peace process, and how this view resonates favorably with Assad, see "Assad: Linchpin of Mideast Peace," *Jerusalem Post*, December 17, 1995. Even as foreign minister, Peres was already building up Syria's regional role and calling it the key to Middle East peace. "If we reach an agreement this time [with Syria]," he said, "it will in fact put an end to the state of war in the Middle East"; see *Los Angeles Times*, May 5, 1995; and *Mideast Mirror*, April 18, 1995.

In the present climate of rapid and revolutionary change in the Middle East, in which Israel seems to be searching for Arab partners with whom to establish a warm peace, Israeli attitudes toward Lebanon are disappointingly stagnant, if not dismissive. Israel has all but written off Lebanon as a lost prospect. Its peace strategies toward Syria are predicated on this gloomy assumption and governed by the incontrovertible reality of Syria's current domination of its hapless neighbor. Though this approach might make some sense as Lebanon remains captive in the short run, it could preclude real opportunities for warm peace looming on the horizon. Watching their country being bargained away unceremoniously has had a devastating psychological effect on the Lebanese, including those inclined to greater warmth in their outlook toward Israel.[39]

---

[39] Some Israelis have noted their country's moral dilemma on this issue. Writing in *Ha'aretz* (December 15, 1995), Joel Marcus commented that: "It is strange that Israel is willing to recognize Assad's regime in Lebanon as one of the components of a settlement. How can a country that is ending decades of occupation lend a hand to perpetuating the rule of another people over another people without dying of shame?"

VI

Conclusions and Policy Recommendations

"Lebanon today may well be the only remaining satellite state in the world."[1] Indeed, Syrian-occupied Lebanon is truly reminiscent of the Cold War era "captive nations"—such as the Baltic states or the Ukraine—under Soviet rule. As the Iron Curtain fades into oblivion around the world, an "iron curtain" of sorts has descended upon Lebanon. Part of the horror this reality evokes comes from the fact that it is taking place and solidifying precisely as the trend of satellite states is receding decisively all over the globe. Lebanon's forced march in reverse—induced by a combination of circumstances, the apathy of some, and the convenience of others—is one of the Middle East's most arresting anachronisms and a key anomaly in the regional peace process.

The lessons to be drawn from Lebanon's "participation" in the Middle East peace process are more akin to general observations and reflections than hard, correlational inferences. Divided societies such as Lebanon, sprung from a heterogeneous communalism, manifest congenital structural weaknesses that no peace agreement alone can fully remedy. At best, peace can create a climate conducive to the laborious, piecemeal reassembly of the fractured state. In Lebanon's case, this will start to occur when Israel and Syria are induced to provide it with a bit of much-needed breathing space.

Despite their differences, the majority of Lebanese share similar sentiments on a number of vital issues—the terrible, destructive consequences of futile intercommunal conflict, the absence of adequate and equitable representation in the country's political institutions, the failure of political parties across the national spectrum, the feeling of alienation from the state, varying degrees of urgency regarding the threats to the country's traditional freedoms, the deterioration of economic conditions—and they all face the future with an unstable mixture of meager hope and much trepidation. Taken together, these points of convergence constitute a shared "anxiety index" that can serve as a modest basis for national reconciliation in an atmosphere founded on the principles of mutual respect and recognition of individual and communal rights and duties.

The Middle East is generally inhospitable and unforgiving when it comes to the survival of delicate, composite entities such as Lebanon,

---

[1] Author interview with Daniel Pipes, Washington, DC, October 1996.

particularly when they manage on brief occasions to break out of the regional mold and glimpse more promising horizons. At the same time, Middle Easterners of all ethnic and political hues yearn for precisely the values and ingredients that differentiate Lebanon from its surroundings: freedom, openness, diversity, novelty, and initiative. Lebanon's weaknesses and strengths raise value-laden questions, and as such are but a mirror and a microcosm of the realities and potentials of the region as a whole. The Arab governments' treatment of a recovering Lebanon in the approaching era of peace will determine the extent to which they are genuinely interested in, and truly receptive to, democratic reform in their own societies.

For its part, Israel will find itself increasingly asking Lebanese-type questions as it settles into a more benign regional order and integrates further into the neighborhood. Lebanon's peculiar pluralism and the complex manner in which its different sub-groups with divergent world views interact and do (or do not) "get along" can offer unique and instructive insights into hitherto elusive aspects of the singular world that is the Middle Eastern bazaar. There are organic linkages between internal developments in Lebanon and the regional dimension of the peace process. Lebanon's marginalization in that process is objectively justified by its lack of independent decisionmaking on two essential components of the peace equation: territory and security. Viewed in terms of its potential as a viable peace interlocutor, Syria is the party that controls Lebanon's territory and security. Therefore, internal developments that tighten or loosen Syria's grip on Lebanon have a direct bearing not only on its status in the negotiations and the shape of any final agreement, but also on Syria's post-peace regional standing. Thus, a great deal hinges on the outcome of the ongoing confrontation between Lebanon's civil society and Syrian hegemony.

In a world in which states operate on the basis of national interests defined primarily in terms of wealth, power, and security, a petroleum-free country like Lebanon does not fare very well. Herein lies the delusion of "neutrality" that the Lebanese have cultivated over the years to their detriment, the hollowness of which has been completely exposed by the war and then by the peace process. Unless neutrality is of the armed variety, it becomes at best a version of "Finlandization" (or some pathetic form of "bufferism") and at worst a synonym for a power vacuum waiting to be filled, which is exactly what Lebanon was until it became a satellite of Syria. If Lebanon's unenviable status in the peace process teaches anything, it is that the country's future viability as an independent, self-determining state depends to an essential degree on its ability to take charge of its own internal security and fulfill its security obligations under regional and international agreements.

Doing so, however, would necessitate stripping Syria of the security excuse that helps keep its forces stationed in Lebanon. At present, Syria enjoys a degree of obstructive veto power over any security-related issue in the country, allowing it to create insecurity and instability at will in order to subvert precisely such bids for self-sufficiency. Given a choice between a free and democratic Lebanon that is less stable and secure, and a secure and stable Lebanon that is less free and democratic, Lebanon's neighbors appear to prefer the latter—despite the fact that a majority of the Lebanese (like any freedom-loving people) would surely opt for the former. Thus, Lebanon's fate rests on the willingness of Jerusalem and Washington to alter the rules of the game so as to reduce—or eliminate—Damascus' capability to manipulate its prized hostage for political and strategic gain.

The range of possible peace process outcomes depends on the degree to which Syria is able to subsume Lebanon under its aegis. If this ongoing assimilation crosses a point of no return, the minimal option will be Israeli withdrawal from South Lebanon in return for security guarantees underwritten by Syria; all else will be consigned indefinitely to the deep freeze of a cold peace. Under no circumstances will Damascus allow Beirut to unilaterally normalize relations with Israel. If, however, Syria falls short of achieving its goals in Lebanon, options closer to the maximal scenario will have a chance of seeing the light of day: accelerated normalization, warmer peace, the rudiments of Lebanon's disengagement from Syria, and restoration of its sovereignty.[2] By definition, it will also mean Syria's return to a less inflated and tractable size.

Any Israel-Lebanon peace scenario will require its own special set of CBMs (confidence-building measures). Since 1982, a crisis of confidence has developed between the two sides that reflects itself, for example, in the uncertainty over the future of the inhabitants of Israel's security zone in southern Lebanon. Israel will have to offer more than reassuring words about the whole question of Lebanon's sovereignty if it hopes to dispel the negative impression that many Lebanese have that it is acquiescing to the Syrian takeover of their country in return for a peace agreement.

BEYOND CARROTS AND STICKS

Without the United States to act as "honest broker and active partner" in what is for all intents and purposes a unipolar world, there would be no Middle East peace process. In regard to Lebanon, three credentials define U.S. impartiality: it is sufficiently removed from the scene, it is not Israel, and it does not behave like Syria. Washington's primary motivators are national security, vital economic and strategic interests, and regional stability (including Israel's security). But it has a morbid fascination with the way the Syrians manage to play Lebanon like an organ. Henry

---

[2] One post-peace danger for Lebanon is the polarization of the Fertile Crescent into two distinct confederations or economic blocs: Israel, Jordan, and the Palestinians on one side and Syria and Lebanon on the other. This would stifle Lebanon's economic prospects and become a recipe for its continued political subservience.

Kissinger's infamous remark about "admiring Assad" encapsulates the prevailing mood. Despite slowly and indefinitely disintegrating in the corrosive acid of Syrian occupation, Lebanon's place in Damascus' custody somehow seems a convenient way to dispose of a painful and peripheral embarrassment.

But Washington is presumably striving for comprehensive regional peace. If the price is Lebanon's continued captivity, it begs the question of whether the outcome of such a process can still be classified as "peace." In an ideal world (at least from Lebanon's standpoint), peace should not only result in the reclamation of Israeli-occupied territory in the south, but also produce clear momentum toward the decoupling of Lebanon and Syria—explicit conditions for the restoration of the country's sovereignty, independence, and eclipsed freedoms. As matters have unfolded thus far, however, the *opposite* momentum is emerging: namely, one that entrenches Syria in Lebanon as a prerequisite for the attainment of a Syrian-Israeli deal. Despite this prevailing trend, the Middle East peace process remains Lebanon's best and perhaps only hope to make a slow recovery to something approaching a normal nation.

To do so, however, one basic condition must be fulfilled. The parties involved—principally the United States—must sincerely adopt a long-term view of Lebanon and its problems that transcends the actual peace process itself. Such an attitude would differentiate between transitory gains and permanent solutions, and take the time to chart specific, incremental, and nearly cost-free steps designed to address Lebanon's circumstances. For this to occur, the parties would have to take Lebanon seriously as an integral entity embodying values consistent with U.S. interests and aspirations, and look beyond the tactical notion of using a combination of carrots and sticks to prod the peace process along toward a utilitarian bilateral arrangement between Israel and Syria.

Lebanon's marginalization during the actual peace negotiations need not conflict with a broader vision of the future that includes a fully revitalized Lebanon in a Middle East that has largely been freed of the specter of the half-century Arab-Israeli conflict. In the absence of such an extended outlook and interim U.S. diplomatic steps, the process of achieving "peace" in the region would do little more for Lebanon than echo the words of contemporary French philosopher and culture critic Jean Baudrillard, who wrote audaciously that the Gulf War did not in fact take place.[3] The same point was expressed somewhat facetiously by the

---

[3] Before, during, and after the Gulf War, Jean Baudrillard wrote three philosophically fascinating articles in which he argued that the "war" was won in advance, and thus "we will never know what it would have been like had it existed." He continues: "We will never know what an Iraqi taking part with a chance of fighting would have been like. We will never know what an American taking part with a chance of being beaten would have been like" (p. 61, English edition); the three articles were subsequently published as a short book entitled *La Guerre du Golfe n'a pas eu lieu* (Paris: Editions Galilee, 1991). For the English

Council of Lebanese American Organizations, a Washington-based lobbying group with grassroots in the American-Lebanese community, when it wrote that Lebanon is being offered "the peace of the grave, rather than the peace of the brave."[4]

For understandable reasons, the question of how to make the Middle East peace process and its outcome more meaningful for Lebanon may not have arisen much lately in U.S. policy circles. Occupied Lebanon is, for the most part, seemingly tranquil; a comprehensive peace agreement between Syria and Israel is expected to address the volatile situation that lingers in the south. Delving more deeply into Lebanon's internal problems—specifically, the multi-faceted showdown that has pitted all components of its beleaguered civil society against Syrian absorption—is not an appetizing proposition for many in Washington.

Direct American attempts undertaken in the recent past to salvage Lebanon produced little and left a distasteful legacy. Conventional wisdom sees 1984 as the crucial turning point for American (dis)involvement in Lebanon's affairs. During the fall of the previous year the devastating suicide bombing of the U.S. Marine barracks near Beirut airport left 243 American soldiers dead. The tragedy jolted Washington policymakers in a manner similar to that experienced by the Israelis in the wake of their own sour Lebanon adventure.[5] The subsequent prolonged agony of innocent American hostages seized in Lebanon reinforced Washington's desire to place distance between itself and anything Lebanese. Henceforth, Lebanon was relegated to the "back burner" of U.S. Middle East policy, where it has remained ever since. The Taif agreement, hailed with American approval as an "Arab solution" to the Lebanon problem, effectively shoved the Lebanon problem onto someone else's shoulders, and stands as stark testimony to waning Western—mainly American—concern. Unbridled Syrian expansionism, the immoderate growth of Saudi influence, and consolidation of Iran-inspired and -financed Islamist militancy were the natural consequences.

On the whole, an undisguised reticence to dwell much on Lebanon's internal situation has pervaded the attitudes of U.S. government officials, in marked contrast to the ongoing scrutiny afforded Iraq.[6] Throughout

---

version, see Jean Baudrillard, *The Gulf War Did Not Take Place*, trans. Paul Patton (Sydney: Power Institute of Fine Arts Publications, 1995).

[4] "Lebanon Must Not be the Sacrificial Lamb at the Middle East Peace Parley," CLAO press release dated January 1, 1996.

[5] American involvement in Lebanon was hesitant and half-hearted even before the bombing. Among the most unfortunate manifestations of this were "rules of engagement" that prohibited Marines guarding the barracks from loading their guns with live ammunition.

[6] This may result in part from deep-seated anti-Maronite prejudices nurtured in what Robert Kaplan calls the "Arabist" camp in American diplomatic circles. With the emergence in recent years of those more sympathetic to Israel at the State Department, the potency of the traditional Arabists has "been diluted," but this has not necessarily resulted in an

most of the Lebanon war, except for the brief phase of direct U.S. and multinational involvement in 1982-83, official American statements on Lebanon generally did not exceed the now hackneyed formula expressing support for "Lebanon's national unity, independence, sovereignty, and territorial integrity."[7] Between the 1982 Israeli invasion and the 1989 Taif accord, occasional American statements spoke of the need for all foreign forces to depart from Lebanon. After Taif, there was less talk of foreign forces leaving, and intermittent statements about the need for Syrian forces to comply with a provision in the agreement to redeploy out of Beirut to eastern Lebanon. As recently as a February 1996 news conference with visiting French President Jacques Chirac, President Clinton made the explicit statement that Lebanon's independence will not be sacrificed in the course of securing a peace agreement between Israel and Syria.

State Department and National Security Council officials are a little more forthcoming, however, when outlining Washington's policy on Lebanon at congressional hearings and in communications with senators, representatives, and other interested parties. They frequently express justified concerns about the continued threat of terrorist attacks against U.S. citizens in Lebanon.[8] In occasional private communications, administration statements on Lebanon are even bolder than these official, publicly stated policy pronouncements.[9]

Many of Lebanon's true and outspoken friends in Washington can be found in the place where totalitarianism and militant fanaticism find no admirers: the United States Congress. At several critical junctures during the war in Lebanon (and following the Taif agreement), senators and representatives of both parties openly proclaimed their outrage at the Syrian occupation and Iranian meddling, and asserted their support for

---

improvement in Lebanon's standing; see Robert D. Kaplan, *The Arabists: The Romance of an American Elite* (New York: The Free Press, 1993), especially pp. 288, 306.

[7] Recitations of this familiar formula (or variations thereof) summarizing the official U.S. position on Lebanon—too numerous to list here—go back to the outbreak of the Lebanon war in 1975.

[8] An example of such candor is the exchange between Assistant Secretary of State for Near Eastern Affairs Robert H. Pelletreau and Representative Lee Hamilton of the House Foreign Relations Committee, who submitted official questions about Lebanon to Mr. Pelletreau on April 6, 1995. See also the letter dated September 13, 1995 from Assistant Secretary of State for Legislative Affairs Wendy R. Sherman to Senator Spencer Abraham, in which she explained the government's reasons for instituting the ban on travel to Lebanon.

[9] One example is a December 1995 letter from Sherman to Rep. Hamilton in which she explicitly states that "no peace in the Middle East will be lasting or comprehensive without an agreement between Israel and an *independent* Lebanon" (emphasis added). This is followed, however, by the realistic qualifier: "But, as important as we hold the freedom and independence of Lebanon, this is not a goal we can pursue in a vacuum." Another example appears in a November 1994 letter from Assistant Secretary Pelletreau to Daniel Nassif, Washington representative of the Council of Lebanese American Organizations, in which Pelletreau stated: "We look forward to the day when Lebanon, at peace with its neighbors and free of all foreign forces, resumes its rightful place among the states of the region."

Lebanon's independence and distinctive values.[10] More concretely, the House of Representatives and Senate have on a few occasions adopted unanimous resolutions urging Syria to adhere to the Taif agreement and withdraw its troops from Beirut as a prelude to complete withdrawal from Lebanon. The resolutions also call upon the president to make future U.S. assistance to Damascus conditional on Syria's departure from Lebanon.[11] Lebanese political clout in America remains minuscule, however, and U.S. geopolitical interests in Lebanon—currently reduced to a vanishing point—are viewed as marginal, so these resolutions do not get translated into policy. Yet their existence and recurrence signal a moral victory for Lebanon's cause in the mind of the American people.

Few Lebanese were so naive in 1983 as to expect the Marines to "save" Lebanon and drive the Syrians and other foreign occupation forces from its soil, and fewer still are foolish enough to entertain seriously such ideas now. For a variety of unsurprising reasons, the possibility of U.S. military intervention on behalf of Lebanon's independence and sovereignty are pure fantasy; Lebanon is not Bosnia. In fact, there is broad agreement among responsible Lebanese that any American military action would be harmful and counterproductive. Yet Lebanon's expectations of the United States over the years have oscillated between the unrealistically fantastic and the equally unrealistically reserved, and it has rarely offered a tempered and reasonable articulation of the specific points of intersection between American interests and its own which do not necessarily entail the kind of direct American involvement that carries a prohibitive political price tag.

Only the United States has the clout to make a tangible difference in Lebanon's favor during the peace negotiations and, more importantly, after the treaties are signed. Moreover, the United States has demonstrated that it is not averse to helping Lebanon when it judges this to be feasible and attainable within the overall parameters of American interests. Washington's preferred course of action on Lebanon appears to be a long-term strategy of sustained incrementalism on a variety of fronts. Meanwhile, Lebanon's strained civil society is busy practicing all of the self-help it can muster on its own in an attempt to ward off the malignant effects of protracted occupation. With the passage of time, however, it is in danger of succumbing to the relentless attrition induced by the pressures of subjugation.

---

[10] Two examples suffice to illustrate bipartisan congressional enthusiasm for a free Lebanon: see Senator Jesse Helms (R–NC), "Syria's Puppet," *Washington Post*, September 1, 1992; and Representative Eliot L. Engel (D–NY), "Syria Foreign Policy Must Change," *Washington Times*, December 29, 1995.

[11] See the Senate of the United States and the House of Representatives (Concurrent Resolution), S. Con. Res. 129 in *Congressional Record* 138, no. 101, July 9, 1992; see also 103d Congress, first session, July 1, 1993, (Concurrent Resolution), S. Con. Res. 28; similarly, see the House of Representatives, "Sense of the Congress Regarding Syrian Occupation of Lebanon," Sec. 2712, June 7, 1995.

RECOMMENDATIONS FOR U.S. POLICY

Lebanon undoubtedly has a long and arduous road to recovery ahead of it. There are no magical remedies. The direction in which history seems inexorably to be heading, however, favors the spread of freedom and democracy while placing dictatorships at an increasing disadvantage. Lebanon's current status as a "captive nation" is therefore unnatural and ultimately untenable, and therein resides hope for its gradual rejuvenation.

The challenge for U.S. policymakers is to develop a course of action that entails effective, catalytic, and nearly cost-free steps aimed at promoting the eventual decoupling of Lebanon from Syria, without impinging upon Syria's vital interests in Lebanon. Defined in reasonable terms that the international community can condone, these "vital" interests would include—but not exceed—solid guarantees of Syrian security, a measure of influence proportional to the historical and fraternal ties between the two states, good neighborliness, and the normal political, economic, and social affinities dictated by geographic proximity and the cultural similarities between the two countries.

Confining Syria's vital interests in Lebanon to these boundaries is naturally complicated by the difference in the political systems of the two countries, by the expansionist—even predatory—ideological disposition of the former *vis-à-vis* the latter, and the realities on the ground in Lebanon. Nevertheless, specific practical suggestions for U.S. policy, which would fall within that narrow region of American political affordability without precipitating an adverse Syrian reaction, are still possible. The following are eight such "safe" suggestions that would greatly bolster the resilience of Lebanon's besieged civil society as it fights for its life against the twin dangers of erosion and assimilation:

- *Encourage the gradual growth of a credible, responsible, and free opposition in the Lebanese body politic.* Such an opposition would constitute neither a artificial creation operating within prescribed guidelines nor a reckless and destabilizing spoiler out to foment unrest and turn back the clock by force. Instead, it would be an authentic opposition with a solid popular base, acting rationally and responsibly in true democratic fashion according to a national agenda designed to strengthen basic freedoms, openness, and pluralist diversity celebrating distinctive communal identities within the sphere of shared aspirations.[12] Elements of such an opposition currently exist within and beyond Lebanon. They cut across religious divisions and need to be encouraged to emerge gradually on the political scene. Giving the leaders and members of this opposition occasional exposure through

---

[12] Using the Taif agreement as an example, such an opposition would neither "rubber stamp" the agreement blindly nor pretend it does not exist. At the same time, it would not confine itself to protesting the disproportionate implementation of the agreement, but would instead be critical of specific provisions in Taif and call for their amendment or abrogation while offering constructive alternatives for debate.

meetings with senior American officials would be useful and not hurt anyone.

• *Focus world attention in advance on Lebanon's year 2000 parliamentary elections in order to help avoid a repetition of the electoral farces of 1992 and 1996.* Four conditions must be satisfied for parliamentary elections to yield something approaching fair results. First, the electoral law must be reformed so that the districts cannot be "gerrymandered" in such a way as to secure the outcome of elections in advance. Smaller, homogeneous districts tend to reflect more accurately the demographic realities and be more representative of the popular will. Innovative ideas such as holding primaries as part of a two-phased election process merit consideration. All Lebanese abroad who are of legal age and who retain valid passports should be granted the right to vote.[13]

Second, all individuals newly naturalized as Lebanese citizens on the basis of the 1994 Naturalization Decree (and any similar decrees subsequently issued by the government and approved by the present parliament) should be barred from voting or running for office for a specific period of time. Third, a provisional government that includes credible representatives of all the main political factions in the country should be formed six months in advance to prepare for and oversee the elections. Finally, impartial international observers should be present to observe the elections.

Serious attempts to fulfill these conditions, encouraged judiciously by the United States, would ensure wide popular participation in the 2000 parliamentary elections—particularly by the Christians, who boycotted the 1992 elections and whose participation in the 1996 elections was generally weak and hesitant. Securing these four conditions would also produce a more representative legislature. Given the ominous precedent established in 1995 by the capricious extension of the president's term in office, less than complete fulfillment of these conditions runs the risk of producing rigged parliaments like those of 1992 and 1996, thereby providing Syria with the additional "legitimacy" it seeks in order to remain in and continue to absorb Lebanon.

• *Maintain high-level condemnation of human rights violations perpetrated by the local authorities and/or foreign forces in Lebanon, and make further aid contingent on tangible improvements in the record.* This can be done in cooperation with local and internationally renowned non-governmental human rights organizations. Authoritarian regimes and their surrogates are generally ill-

---

[13] One glaring defect of the present system is that, although seats in the parliament are apportioned among the religious sects and denominations, representatives are chosen by a mixed electorate rather than exclusively by members of their own religious community. As a result, certain communities' representation is distorted by their demographic concentration and geographic dispersion. To avoid this, the electoral law should stipulate that each community elect its own representatives to parliament regardless of geography. This would assuage communal fears of false or underrepresentation, and in turn create an atmosphere better suited to real coexistence.

equipped to comprehend the debilitating cumulative effect that recurrent public exposure and condemnation have on their ability to use repression, torture, and brutality as instruments of policy. Exploiting this blind spot can make an imperceptible yet real difference on the ground by giving Lebanon's battered civil society a fighting chance. This approach has been empirically tested and proven effective in Lebanon and communist Eastern Europe, especially when the United States was seen to be genuinely concerned.

- *Lend moral and other support to autonomous institutions that fortify Lebanese civil society.* These components include the country's market economy, free press, independent judiciary, unions and professional associations (e.g., labor, students, physicians, engineers, lawyers, teachers), the public and private educational sector, women's groups, credible NGOs, and others. Reinforcing Lebanon's societal diversity and initiative (sometimes a mere official public statement would suffice) revives and anchors its dynamic pluralism, which in turn gives it a better chance of outlasting monolithic, authoritarian, and centralized systems. A vibrant civil society is the best antidote to the religious fanaticism and militant extremism that breed terrorism, and the best American investment for the long term.

- *Build the Lebanese armed forces, not as a tool of government repression, but as an independent and patriotic institution capable of taking responsibility for security.* Through targeted American programs, conditional aid, and restructuring that encourages its patriotic elements, the Lebanese army and related security forces can gradually begin to assume a greater and more effective responsibility for national defense and internal security. A revamped Lebanese army whose reach extends all the way to the international border must constitute an integral part of the final settlement leading to an Israeli withdrawal from its self-declared security zone.

Four basic requirements have to be fulfilled in order to stabilize the situation in southern Lebanon. First, the SLA should gradually be integrated into the Lebanese army. This can commence with the creation of a joint liaison committee comprised of officers from both organizations to oversee security in the south. The Beirut authorities' spurious charges against specific individuals in the SLA should be dropped in the same way that similar charges were not pressed against collaborators with other foreign powers elsewhere in Lebanon.

Second, a sizable multinational peacekeeping force (not necessarily including U.S. troops) may need to be stationed in southern Lebanon for a defined period of time with a specific mandate to assist the Lebanese army in assuming full responsibility for security in the area. Together, these forces would patrol the international border, ensure Lebanese compliance with all international agreements, provide protection against the possibility of reprisals directed at the civilian inhabitants of the former Israeli security zone, and maintain overall security in the south.

Third, Hezbollah's military wing and other such independent militias would be disarmed and disbanded, as occurred with virtually all other armed groups after the Lebanon war. This would include the removal from Lebanon of any Iranian Revolutionary Guards. Finally, as part of the final agreements between Israel and Syria/Lebanon, Syrian forces would be prohibited from entering southern Lebanon for any reason.

The Syria-Lebanon security agreement would continue to be respected and upheld while the enhancement and restructuring of the Lebanese army was underway. These requirements would not conflict with most provisions of the security agreement, but would take precedence over it in the event of a conflict between the agreement and reform efforts.

- *Insist on implementation of the Taif agreement clause that requires Syrian forces to redeploy from the greater Beirut area to the Bekaa Valley and other points east.* This would restore some very important symbolic balance to the way Taif has been implemented so far, though it would leave in place the largely unseen Syrian security and intelligence network and the hundreds of thousands of Syrian workers spread throughout the country.

- *Modify the American attitude toward Taif to allow substantive amendments to the agreement to be introduced and debated in a new and freely elected parliament.* The imbalance inherent in the Taif agreement as a purely "Arab" initiative should be rectified by reintroducing more vigorous direct Western engagement (i.e., the United States, France, Germany, the Vatican) in the formation of a final internal settlement for Lebanon. After Middle East peace, there will be no reason for continued Western abdication of involvement in the affairs and destiny of Lebanon. Rather than a final, irrevocable document, Taif should be seen as an interim step to a more permanent, just, and equitable national pact—and, more importantly, a federal political formula—between the Muslim (and particularly Shi'a) and Christian communities that would take into account their qualitatively different levels of grievance and existential fear and provide constitutionally grounded guarantees of the rights and freedoms of all individuals and religious communities in the country, regardless of fluctuating demographics.

- *Urge rapid normalization of relations between Lebanon and Israel once a formal peace treaty has been signed.* Under the proper conditions, this could lay the foundation for a truly warm peace similar to (if not surpassing) that which Israel already enjoys with Jordan. Circumventing preemptive, pseudo-legal restrictions against normalization that are embedded in the numerous bilateral agreements Syria has imposed on Lebanon will be difficult, but not impossible. Nothing undermines closed societies more than the fresh air of transparency. The United States should use its role as the champion of open markets to insist, for example, on the deregulation and privatization of Lebanon's archaic telecommunications sector, and then assist in upgrading it to Western standards. Getting Lebanon "on line" would help expose many of the hegemonic measures being inflicted on it.

Similarly, energizing the other sectors of the Lebanese economy would wean it away from plutocratic monopolies and toward *laissez-faire* entrepreneurialism that will enhance the prosperity of the middle class, the pillar of stability in all healthy societies. An economically thriving Lebanon would pose little threat to either Israel or Syria. Lebanon will never rival, or even compete with, Israel in terms of high-technology; on the contrary, the future portends complementary economic roles. By the same token, the resurrection of Lebanon's traditionally independent and flourishing free enterprise economy is Syria's surest and fastest means to a brighter economic future unshackled by obsolete centralism.

To remain stable and prosper, Lebanon's emerging anti-war consensus must be transformed into a consensus for peaceful coexistence and cooperation in nation-building. This will begin only when it is surrounded by socio-cultural and communal autonomy. A unique feature of Lebanon in the twentieth century has always been its rich communal diversity within an overall unified state structure. Through a simultaneous emphasis on distinctiveness and interaction, individuals and the autonomous communities to which they belong are both able to engage in dynamic self-actualization in nearly any creative direction.

As they strive to remold their common bonds as a people, the challenge facing the Lebanese is to calibrate the optimal relationship between center and periphery; preserve healthy heterogeneity, variety, and multiplicity while promoting a shared sense of solidarity, civic awareness, and participatory citizenship within a single unified Lebanon; and determine the precise degree of decentralization that would best protect distinctiveness without leading to fragmentation and disintegration—in short, to balance the complex centripetal and centrifugal forces that act concurrently on them as a people. Their future relations with their immediate neighbors, Syria and Israel, will depend first and foremost on the efforts they make internally to accept each other as they are.

In the face of difficult odds, the Lebanese have begun to take the first courageous steps toward rallying their civil society. It is time the rest of the region and the world looked upon their efforts approvingly and lent a hand.

Appendices

NATIONAL RECONCILIATION (TAIF) ACCORD
October 22, 1989

General Principles and Reforms

I. <u>General Principles</u>

A. Lebanon is a sovereign, free, and independent country; a final homeland for all of its citizens; a unity of people, land, and institutions within its borders as defined by the Lebanese constitution and recognized internationally.

B. Lebanon is of Arab affiliation and identity; it is a founding and active member of the Arab League and is bound by its charter; it is a founding and active member of the United Nations and abides by its charter, and it is a member of the Non-Aligned Movement. The Lebanese state manifests these principles in all fields and domains without exception.

C. Lebanon is a democratic, parliamentary republic founded on the respect for public liberties, the foremost of which are freedom of opinion and belief, and on social justice and equality of rights and duties among all citizens without discrimination or distinction.

D. The people are the source of power and the possessors of sovereignty which they exercise through the constitutional institutions.

E. The system is founded on the principle of separation, balance, and cooperation of powers.

F. The economic system is a free system that assures individual initiative and private ownership.

G. The balanced cultural, social, and economic growth of the region is a principal pillar of the pillars of unity of the state and of the stability of the system.

H. To seek the realization of comprehensive social justice through financial, economic and social reforms.

I. The land of Lebanon is but one land for all Lebanese; and every Lebanese has the right to reside on any part thereof and to enjoy it under the supremacy of the law. No segregation of people on the basis of any affiliation whatsoever: no partitioning, dividing, or settling.

J. No legitimacy to any authority that contradicts the charter of cohabitation.

II. Political Reforms

A. Parliament

Parliament is the legislative authority; it exercises comprehensive control over the policy of government and its affairs.

1. The head of parliament and his deputy are elected for the duration of the term of parliament.

2. Two years following the election of the head of parliament and his deputy, and in the first meeting it holds, parliament may, for one time only, withdraw its confidence from the head of parliament or his deputy by a two-thirds majority of its members pursuant to a petition signed by at least ten deputies. Parliament must immediately in this case hold a meeting to fill in the vacant position.

3. Each project law referred to parliament by the Council of Ministers that is classified as urgent shall not be issued except, after being listed on the agenda of a regular session and read therein, after the passage of the time delay mentioned in the constitution, without being acted upon and after the approval of the Council of Ministers.

4. The electoral unit is the *mohafazah*.

5. Until parliament enacts an election law which is not based on religious affiliation, seats in parliament shall be allocated according to the following rule:

   a. Equally between Christians and Muslims.

   b. Proportionally among the sects of each of the two categories.

   c. Proportionally among the regions.

6. The number of members of parliament shall be increased to (108), divided equally between Christians and Muslims. The newly created positions based on the present charter, as well as the positions which became vacant prior to its declaration shall, for once and by exception, be filled in by appointment of the anticipated government of national reconciliation.

7. Concurrent with the election of the first parliament on a national rather than confessional basis, a Senate will be created wherein all spiritual families will be represented with its authority being confined to matters of destiny.

B. The President of the Republic

The president of the republic is the head of the state and the symbol of the unity of the nation; he undertakes to secure the integrity of the constitution and to preserve the independence of Lebanon, its unity, and the safety of its land as mandated by the constitution. He is the supreme commander of the armed forces, subject to the authority of the Council of Ministers. The president exercises the following authorities:

1. He chairs the Council of Ministers at his discretion without voting.

2. He heads the Supreme Council of Defense.

3. He issues the decrees and requests their proclamation. He has the right to ask the Council of Ministers to re-consider any decision taken by it within a period of fifteen days from the time said decision is deposited with the presidency. If the Council of Ministers insists on the decision taken, or if the delay has passed without the decree being issued or returned, the decree or the decision becomes imperatively effective and must be proclaimed.

4. He issues the laws as per the delays stipulated by the constitution, and requests their proclamation following their ratification by parliament. He has the right, following notification of the Council of Ministers, to demand the reconsideration of a [new] law within the delays stipulated by the constitution and in conformity with its mandates; and in the event the delays end without their issue or return, the law becomes imperatively effective and must be proclaimed.

5. He refers project laws, submitted to him by the Council of Ministers, to parliament.

6. He nominates the designated prime minister in consultation with the head of parliament based on binding parliamentary consultations that he officially communicates to the head of parliament

7. He individually issues the decree nominating the prime minister.

8. He issues, in agreement with the prime minister, the decree constituting the government.

9. He issues the decrees accepting the resignation of the government or the resignation or dismissal of ministers.

10. He accredits ambassadors and accepts their credentials, and awards official state decorations by decree.

11. He assumes negotiation in entering into international treaties and their execution in agreement with the prime minister; such treaties do not become effective except after the consent of the Council of Ministers; the government shall, whenever national interest and the safety of the state permit, present them to parliament. As to treaties comprising terms that are related to state finance and commercial agreements and other agreements which may not be abrogated on a year-to-year basis, they must not be executed except by consent of parliament.

12. He addresses, when necessary, letters to parliament.

13. He calls parliament, in agreement with the prime minister and pursuant to a decree, into extraordinary sessions.

14. The president has the right to present to the Council of Ministers any emergency issue not included on the meeting agenda.

15. He exceptionally convenes the Council of Ministers, as he deems it necessary, in agreement with the prime minister.

16. He grants private pardons by decree.

17. The president shall not bear the consequences of carrying out his functions, except when violating the constitution or in the case of high treason.

C. The Prime Minister

The prime minister is the head of government, he represents it and speaks on its behalf, and is considered responsible for the implementation of the general policy established by the Council of Ministers. He exercises the following authorities:

1. He heads the Council of Ministers.

2. He conducts parliamentary consultations to form the government and signs with the president the decree for its constitution. The government shall, within a period of thirty days, present its ministerial address to parliament to obtain its confidence; and it shall not exercise its authorities prior to acquiring the confidence of parliament, or following its resignation or being deemed resigned, except in the narrow meaning of carrying out business.

3. He presents to parliament the general policy of government.

4. He signs all decrees, except the decree designating the prime minister and the decree accepting the resignation of the government or deeming it resigned.

5. He signs the decree calling for an extraordinary session and the decrees proclaiming the laws and the request for their reconsideration.

6. He calls on the Council of Ministers to convene and draws up its meeting agenda; and informs the president, *a priori*, of the subjects included thereon as well as of the urgent matters that will be discussed, and signs the original minutes of meetings.

7. He follows up the activities of the departments and public agencies and coordinates among the ministers, and gives general directives so as to ensure a proper flow of work.

8. He holds, in the presence of the minister concerned, working sessions with involved parties in the state.

9. He is, imperatively, the deputy head of the Supreme Council of Defense.

D. The Council of Ministers

The executive power is vested in the Council of Ministers, and among the powers it exercises are the following:

1. Formulating the general policy of the state in all domains, drawing out project laws and decrees and taking necessary decisions for their implementation.

2. Overseeing the implementation of laws and regulations and supervising the activities of all state agencies with no exception, including departments and civil, military, and security institutions.

3. The Council of Ministers is the authority to which the armed forces are subject.

4. Appointing state employees, dismissing them, and accepting their resignation in accordance with the law.

5. The right to dissolve parliament pursuant to a request by the president, if parliament has abstained from meeting during the term of a regular or extraordinary session extending for a period of not less than one month, despite being called in two consecutive times, or if it rejects the national budget in its totality for the purpose of disrupting government activities. The exercise of this right may not be repeated for the same reasons that resulted in the dissolution of parliament the first time.

6. If present, the president heads the meetings of the Council of Ministers. The Council of Ministers convenes regularly in a specific quarter, and the legal quorum for its meeting shall be a two-thirds majority of its members; and it takes its decisions by consensus, and in the absence of consensus, they are taken by voting. Decisions are taken by simple majority of the attendants, except major issues which require the consent of two-thirds of the Council's members. The following subjects are considered major issues:

The state of emergency and lifting it; war and peace; general mobilization; international treaties and agreements; the national budget of the state; comprehensive development and long-range plans; appointment of the employees of the first category and its equivalent; reconsideration of administrative divisions; the dissolution of parliament; elections law; naturalization law; personal statutes laws; the dismissal of ministers.

E. The Minister

The authority of the minister shall be strengthened in line with the general policy of government and the principle of collective responsibility, and he shall not be dismissed except by a decision by the Council of Ministers or by parliament withdrawing confidence from him individually.

F. Resignation of Government, Deeming It Resigned, and Dismissal of Ministers

1. The government shall be considered resigned in the following cases:

   a. If the prime minister has resigned.

   b. If it loses more than one-third of the number of its members specified in the decree constituting it.

   c. Upon the death of its head.

   d. At the commencement of a presidential term.

   e. At the commencement of a parliamentary term.

   f. Upon losing the confidence of parliament as a result or the latter's initiative or by pledging it itself.

2. The dismissal of a minister shall be pursuant to a decree signed by the president and the prime minister following the approval of the Council of Ministers.

3. Upon the resignation of government or deeming it resigned, parliament shall enter into an extraordinary meeting session until a new government has been formed and obtained confidence.

G. Political Deconfessionalization

Political deconfessionalization is a principal national objective that must be pursued in accordance with a transitional plan. Parliament, which is elected on the basis of an equal distribution of Muslims and Christians, shall take appropriate measures to achieve this objective and to form a national commission headed by the President and comprising political, intellectual and societal personalities in addition to the head of parliament and the prime minister. The mission of the commission is to study and recommend the means of eliminating confessionalism and to present them to parliament and to the Council of Ministers and to follow up the implementation of the transitional plan.

During the transitional stage, the following shall be achieved:

1. The rule of confessional representation shall be abolished and qualification and specialization shall be adopted in public offices, the judiciary, the military and security establishments, public and mixed agencies, and independent authorities as may be required to achieve national reconciliation, except for first category positions and their equivalent positions therein, which shall be shared equally by Christians and Muslims with no position being confined to either sect.

2. Abolishing the mention of religion and sect on national identity cards.

III. Other Reforms

A. Administrative Decentralization

1. The Lebanese state is a single unified state with a powerful centralized authority.

2. The authority of governors and of deputy governors shall be extended and all the departments of the state shall be represented in the administrative regions at the highest level possible so as to facilitate the provision of services to the citizens and respond locally to their needs.

3. Reconsidering administrative divisions so as to secure national fusion and preserve cohabitation and the unity of land, people, and institutions.

4. Adopting maximum administrative decentralization on the level of small administrative units (*Kada'* and below) by electing a council for each *Kada'* headed by a deputy governor so as to ensure local participation.

5. Adopting a unified development plan encompassing the nation and enabling the economic and social development of all Lebanese regions, and strengthening the resources of the municipalities, the unified municipalities and the municipality unions with necessary financial means.

B. The Courts

1. In order to secure the submission of all officials and citizens to the supremacy of the law and to secure the conformity of the legislative and executive authorities to the postulate of cohabitation and to the basic rights of the Lebanese citizens stipulated in the constitution:

a. The Supreme Council stipulated in the constitution shall be formed with its mission being the impeachment of presidents and ministers. A special law devoted to the council's legal proceedings shall be decreed.

b. A Constitutional Council shall be established for the purpose of interpreting the constitution and of monitoring the constitutionality of the laws and to rule on all disputes and appeals relating to parliament and Presidential elections.

c. The following parties have the right to consult with the Constitutional Council regarding the interpretation of the constitution and the monitoring of the constitutionality of the laws:

1. The president of the republic.

2. The head of parliament.

3. The prime minister.

d. A certain percentage of the members of parliament.

2. To safeguard the principle of harmony between religion and state, the head of the Lebanese factions shall have the right to consult with the Constitutional Council with regard to:

a. Personal statutes.

b. The freedom of belief and practice of religious rites.

c. Freedom of religious education.

3. To strengthen the independence of the judiciary, a determined number of the members of the Supreme Council of Justice shall be elected by the judicial body.

C. The Law of Parliamentary Elections

Parliamentary elections shall be conducted in accordance with a new election law based on the Governorate (*Mohafazah*) and that considers the principles that guarantee cohabitation among Lebanese and that insures the accuracy of political representation of the various categories of people and their generations and the effectiveness of such representation, after the reconsideration of administrative divisions within the framework of the unity of land, people, and institutions.

D. The Establishment of the Economic and Social Council for Development

A Social Economic Council shall be established to ensure the participation of the representatives of various sectors in the formulation of the economic and social policy of the state by offering advice and suggestions.

E. Education and Instruction

1. To put education at the disposal of people and to make it mandatory, at least in the elementary stage.

2. To emphasize the freedom of education in accordance with the law and regulations.

3. To protect private education and strengthen state control over private schools and the school textbooks.

4. To rehabilitate formal, vocational, and technical education and strengthen and to develop it in such a manner so as to fulfill and suit the developmental and constructive needs of the nation. To rehabilitate the Lebanese University and support it, especially in its applied faculties.

5. To review and develop the curricula in a manner that strengthens national cohesiveness and fusion, and spiritual and cultural openness, and to standardize the textbooks in the history and civil education courses.

J. Information

To reorganize all media under the law and within the framework of responsible freedom, and in a manner that serves the objectives of reconciliation and of ending the state of war.

Reinstating the Sovereignty of the Lebanese State over the Entire Lebanese Land

Whereas an agreement was reached among the Lebanese parties on the establishment of a strong and able state founded on national reconciliation, the government of national reconciliation shall draw up a detailed one-year security plan aiming at gradually reinstating the authority of the Lebanese state over its entire territory by means of its own forces, with its broad lines being characterized as follows:

1. Disbanding all Lebanese and non-Lebanese militias and surrendering their arms to the Lebanese state within a period of six months after the ratification of the National Reconciliation Charter, the election of the president, the formation of the government of national reconciliation, and the adoption of political reform in a constitutional manner.

2. Reinforcing Internal Security Forces through:

   a. Opening the door to all Lebanese, without exception, to volunteer and commence their training centrally and then to distribute them to the units in the *mohafazat*, and to subject them to periodic and organized training programs.

   b. Strengthening the security system in such a way so as to be capable of controlling the entry and exit of persons across land, sea, and air borders.

3. Reinforcing the Armed Forces:

   a. The primary duty of the armed forces is to defend the nation and, if necessary, to protect national order whenever the danger exceeds the capability of the internal security forces to deal with it.

   b. The armed forces shall be used to support the internal security forces in preserving security under circumstances as may be determined by the Council of Ministers.

   c. The armed forces shall be unified, prepared, and trained so as to be capable of assuming its national duties in facing Israeli aggression.

   d. The armed forces shall return to barracks at the time when the internal security forces become ready to assume its security mission.

e. The intelligence activities of the armed forces shall be re-organized to serve military purposes only.

4. Fundamentally solving the problem of the Lebanese immigrants by approving the right of every Lebanese immigrant who emigrated since 1975 to return to the place from which he or she emigrated; passing the necessary legislation securing this right and providing the necessary means for reconstruction.

Whereas the aim of the Lebanese state is to reinstate its authority over the entire Lebanese territory by means of its own forces, which are represented primarily by the internal security forces, and out of the brotherly ties that bind Syria to Lebanon, Syrian forces shall, with due thanks, assist legitimate Lebanese forces in reinstating the sovereignty of the Lebanese state within a maximum of two years after the ratification of the National Reconciliation Charter, the election of the President, the formation of the government of national reconciliation and the adoption of political reforms in a constitutional manner. At the end of this period, the Syrian government and the Lebanese government of national reconciliation will decide on the repositioning of Syrian forces in the Bekaa area and the access to western Bekaa in Dahr-Elbeidar up to the Hamana-Mdeirej-Ein Darah line and, if necessary, other points to be decided by a joint Lebanese-Syrian military committee. Also, an agreement shall be signed by both governments which determines the size and duration of the presence of the Syrian forces in the above areas and the relation of these forces with the Lebanese state authorities present in these areas. The Tripartite Supreme Arab Committee is ready to assist the two states in reaching this agreement, if they so desire.

The Liberation of Lebanon from Israeli Occupation

Regaining the authority of the state up to internationally recognized Lebanese borders requires the following:

1. Pursuing the implementation of UN Resolution 425 and all Security Council resolutions promulgating the total elimination of the Israeli occupation.

2. Adhering to the truce agreement signed on March 23, 1949.

3. Taking all necessary measures to liberate all Lebanese territory from the Israeli occupation, extending the authority of the state over all of its land, deploying the Lebanese army along the internationally recognized borders and pursuing the reinforcement of the existence of the international peacekeeping forces in southern Lebanon so as to ensure the withdrawal of Israel and allow for the return of law and order to the border zone.

Lebanese-Syrian Relations

Lebanon, a country of Arab affiliation and identity, is tied to all Arab states by true fraternal relations; and there exists between Lebanon and Syria distinguished relationships which draw their strength from the roots of kinship, history, and common fraternal interests, which is the concept on which the coordination and cooperation between both countries are and will be manifested in agreements between them in various domains, and in the manner which serves the interests of both countries within the framework of the sovereignty and independence of each of them. Based on that, and because strengthening the bases of security provides the needed atmosphere for the development of these distinguished ties, Lebanon shall under no circumstances be made a source of threat to the security of Syria. And Syria, which is keen on preserving the security, independence, and unity of Lebanon and concurrence among its people, shall not permit of any act which may threaten Lebanon's security, sovereignty, and independence.

TREATY OF BROTHERHOOD, COOPERATION, AND COORDINATION
May 22, 1991

The Lebanese Republic and the Syrian Arab Republic:

By virtue of the distinctive brotherly ties that bind them and that derive their strength from the roots of kinship, history, single affiliation, common destiny, and common interests;

Convinced that achievement of the widest scope of cooperation and coordination would serve their interests, provide the means to guarantee their development and progress, the protection of their national security, provide prosperity and stability, enable them to confront all regional and international developments and meet the aspirations of the peoples of the two states in keeping with the Lebanese National Charter approved by the Council of Deputies on May 11, 1989; Agree on the following:

Article I

The two states will strive to realize the highest degree of cooperation and coordination between them in all political, security, cultural, scientific, and other concerns in pursuit of the interests of the two brotherly countries within the framework of the sovereignty and independence of each of them, so as to enable the two countries to utilize their political, economic, and security resources, guarantee their national security, and expand and strengthen their common interests in affirmation of brotherly relations and for the preservation of their common destiny.

Article II

The two states will strive to achieve cooperation and coordination between the two countries in the fields of economics, agriculture, industry, commerce, transportation, communications, customs, the initiation of joint projects, and the coordination of development plans.

Article III

The inter-relationship of the two countries' security requires that Lebanon not be made the source of a threat to Syria's security, or Syria to Lebanon's, in any circumstance whatsoever. Lebanon shall therefore not allow itself to be a passageway or a base for any power or state or organization the purpose of which is the violation of its security, independence, and sovereignty, or that of Syria.

Article IV

After the approval of the political reforms in a constitutional manner, as the Lebanese National Charter provides, and when the periods specified in the charter expire, the Syrian and Lebanese governments shall decide to redeploy the Syrian forces in the Bekaa region and the Bekaa's western approach in

Dahr el-Baider and up to the Hammana-Mdairej-Ain Dara line and, if necessary, in other posts to be determined through a joint Lebanese-Syrian military committee. The two governments shall also arrive at an agreement that determines the size of the Syrian forces and the duration of their presence in the aforementioned areas, and also determines the relationship of those forces with the authorities of the Lebanese state in the areas where they are present.

Article V

The two countries' foreign policies, both Arab and international, shall be based on the following principles:

1. Lebanon and Syria are two Arab countries committed to the charter of the League of Arab States, the Arab joint Defence and Economic Cooperation Treaty, and all other agreements promulgated in the framework of the League. They are also members of the United Nations, committed to its Charter, and members of the Non-Aligned Movement.

2. The common destiny and common interests of the two countries.

3. Each will support the other in matters relating to its security and its national interests, in keeping with the provisions of this treaty.

The governments of the two countries shall therefore strive to coordinate their Arab and international policies, realize the greatest possible cooperation in Arab and international institutions and organizations, and coordinate their positions on the various regional and international issues.

Article VI

The following agencies shall be instituted to achieve the objectives of this treaty, and other agencies can be established by a decision by the Higher Council mentioned below:

1. The Higher Council

    A. The Higher Council shall be comprised of the president of the republic of each of the two contracting states and the Speaker of the People's Council [parliament], the prime minister and the deputy prime minister of the Syrian Arab Republic; the speaker of the Council of Deputies, the prime minister and the deputy prime minister of the Lebanese Republic.

    B. The Higher Council shall meet once a year and when the need arises, the venue to be agreed upon.

    C. The Higher Council shall define the general policy for coordination and cooperation between the two states in the political, economic, security, military, and other fields and shall oversee its implementation. It shall also approve the plans and decisions of the Follow-up and Coordination Committee, the Foreign

Affairs Committee, the Economic and Social Affairs Committee, and any other committee that may be created later.

D. The decisions of the Higher Council are binding and applicable within the framework of each of the two countries' Constitutional rules.

E. The Higher Council shall determine the topics on which the specialized committees are authorized to make decisions that are automatically implementable in accordance with the Constitutional rules and principles in each of the two countries or if they do not conflict with those rules and principles.

2. The Follow-up and Coordination Committee

The Follow-up and Coordination Committee shall be comprised of the prime ministers of the two countries and a number of ministers concerned with relations between them, and it shall have the following tasks:

A. Following up the implementation of the decisions of the Higher Council and reporting to the Council on the stages of implementation.

B. Coordinating the recommendations and decisions of the specialized committees and referring the suggestions to the Higher Council.

C. Holding meetings with the specialized committees when necessary.

D. The Commission shall meet once every six months and whenever the need arises, the venue to be agreed upon.

3. The Foreign Affairs Committee

A. The Foreign Affairs Committee shall be comprised of the Foreign ministers of the two countries.

B. The Foreign Affairs Committee shall meet once every two months and whenever the need arises, in one of the two countries in rotation.

C. The Foreign Affairs Committee shall strive to coordinate the foreign policies of the two states in their relations with all states, and shall also strive to coordinate their activities and positions in the Arab and international organizations and shall, for that purpose, prepare plans for approval by the Higher Council.

4. The Economic and Social Affairs Committee

A. The Economic and Social Affairs committee shall be comprised of the ministers concerned with the economic and social sectors in the two countries.

B. The Economic and Social Affairs Committee shall meet in one of the two countries in rotation once every two months and whenever the need arises.

C. The task of the Economic and Social Affairs Committee shall be to strive for economic and social coordination between the two states and to prepare recommendations to that end.

D. The recommendations of the Economic and Social Affairs Committee shall go into effect, in keeping with the constitutional principles of each of the two countries, when they are approved by the Higher Council.

5. The Defence and Security Affairs Committee

A. The Defence and Security Affairs Committee shall be comprised of the ministers of Defence and the Interior in each of the two countries.

B. The task of the Defence and Security Committee shall be to study the means by which the two states' security can be preserved and to propose joint measures to confront any aggression or threat to their national security or any disturbances that jeopardize the internal security of either state.

C. All plans and recommendations prepared by the Defence and Security Affairs Committee shall be referred to the Higher Council for approval, in keeping with the Constitutional principles of each of the two countries.

6. The Secretariat General

A. A Secretariat General shall be set up to follow up the implementation of the provisions of this treaty.

B. The Secretariat General shall be headed by a Secretary General appointed by a Higher Council decision.

C. The headquarters, jurisdiction, staff, and budget of the Secretariat General shall be determined by a Higher Council decision.

<u>Final Rules</u>

1. Special agreements shall be signed by the two countries in the fields covered by this treaty—such as the economic, security, defense, and other fields—in accordance with the constitutional principles of each of the two countries, and these shall be considered a complementary part of this treaty.

2. This treaty shall go into effect when it is promulgated by the authorities concerned in accordance with the constitutional principles of the two contracting states.

3. Each of the two states shall take action to annul laws and regulations that are not in conformity with this treaty, without violating the rules of each of the two countries' constitutions.

DEFENSE AND SECURITY AGREEMENT
September 1, 1991

Based on the Brotherhood, Cooperation, and Coordination Treaty between the Lebanese Republic and the Syrian Arab Republic signed in Damascus on May 22, 1991 and ratified by the Lebanese Chamber of Deputies on May 27, 1991 in Beirut, including its third, fifth, and sixth Articles, particularly Clause 5 of the sixth Article, agreement has been reached on the following:

1. Structure

A defense affairs committee consisting of the two countries' defense and interior ministers is to be formed. This committee will meet every three months, alternating between the capital cities of Beirut and Damascus or in any other location agreed upon, and will also meet whenever it is deemed necessary. The committee may seek assistance from any of the chiefs of the two countries' security authorities or from the chiefs of other branches of the two ministries. The army commands, the security services, and other concerned administrative departments will meet every month, alternating between the capital cities and will meet whenever the need arises at an agreed-upon location to implement the defense and security committees' programs and supervise their details.

2. Missions

The defense and security affairs committee is charged with studying ways to safeguard the two states' security and with proposing joint plans to confront any aggression or threat against their national security and any disturbance that may upset either country's internal security.

In implementing the contents of Article III of the Brotherhood, Cooperation, and Coordination Treaty, the following must be realized:

In an effort to reaffirm the two states' pledge and ensure that Lebanon does not become a source of threats against Syria's security and vice versa, the military and security authorities in the two countries must implement the following:

A. Ban all military, security, political, and media activity that might harm the other country.

B. Refuse to give refuge to, facilitate the passage of, or provide protection to persons and organizations that work against the other state's security. If such persons or organizations take refuge in either of the two states, that state must arrest them and hand them over to the other side at the latter's request.

C. To enable the military and security services in each of the two states to carry out their duty of implementing the aforementioned Clauses A and B, these services must meet regularly in each of the two countries to exchange information involving all issues of strategic, national, and internal security, including those related to drugs, major financial crimes, terrorism, and espionage. The military and security services will coordinate their work to follow up and resolve these issues within each country as well as abroad, and will cooperate with international institutions as necessary. All legal and procedural steps must be taken to facilitate the joint action of the two states' authorities as part of the agreement to expedite the adoption of legal prosecution and ways to solve these problems.

D. The two countries' defense ministries and their relevant departments will meet every three months, alternating between the capital cities, and as necessary, to exchange information on everything that concerns the two countries' security and all hostile activities in an effort to reach a mutual understanding on the dangers and their dimensions, and, consequently, to draw up integrated plans at various levels to confront these dangers. In this regard, the two Defense Ministries will establish joint organs to follow up and supervise strategic coordination

E. The two countries' Ministries of Defense and Interior will increase the exchange of officers and troops through training courses at various levels, including the exchange of military instructors in the military colleges, in order to achieve a high standard in military coordination and adequate familiarity to confront common threats.

F. The ministerial committee for defense and security affairs will draw up the necessary plans to promote exchange and development in each country's civil defense field.

3. Final Provisions

In addition to its tasks, the defense and security committee will do the following:

—Follow up the implementation of all the provisions of the agreement and give the necessary instructions to ensure its progress.

—Propose to the Higher Council the bases, principles, and regulations that are bound to ensure full and effective implementation of the agreement.

THE WASHINGTON INSTITUTE POLICY PAPER SERIES

#44: *Iran's Economic Morass: Mismanagement and Decline under the Islamic Republic* by Eliyahu Kanovsky

#43: *Revolution at a Crossroads: Iranian Domestic Politics and Regional Ambitions* by David Menashri

#42: *Iranian Military Power: Capabilities and Intentions* by Michael Eisenstadt

#41: *Partner or Pariah? Attitudes Toward Israel in Syria, Lebanon, and Jordan* by Hilal Khashan

#40: *Syria Beyond the Peace Process* by Daniel Pipes

#39: *Between Pragmatism and Ideology: The Muslim Brotherhood in Jordan, 1989-1994* by Sabah el-Said

#38: *The Economy of Saudi Arabia: Troubled Present, Grim Future* by Eliyahu Kanovsky

#37: *After King Fahd: Succession in Saudi Arabia* by Simon Henderson

#36: *Like a Phoenix from the Ashes? The Future of Iraqi Military Power* by Michael Eisenstadt

#35: *Radical Middle East States and U.S. Policy* by Barry Rubin

#34: *Peace with Security: Israel's Minimal Security Requirements in Negotiations with Syria* by Ze'ev Schiff

#33: *Iran's Challenge to the West: How, When, and Why* by Patrick Clawson

#32: *"The Arab Street?" Public Opinion in the Arab World* by David Pollock

#31: *Arming for Peace? Syria's Elusive Quest for "Strategic Parity"* by Michael Eisenstadt

#30: *The Economic Consequences of the Persian Gulf War: Accelerating OPEC's Demise* by Eliyahu Kanovsky

#29: *King Hussein's Strategy of Survival* by Uriel Dann

#28: *The Arrow Next Time? Israel's Missile Defense Program for the 1990s* by Marvin Feuerwerger

#27: *Palestinian Self-Government (Autonomy): Its Past and Its Future* by Harvey Sicherman

#26: *Damascus Courts the West: Syrian Politics, 1989-1991* by Daniel Pipes

#25: *Economic Consequences of Peace for Israel, the Palestinians, and Jordan* by Patrick Clawson and Howard Rosen

#24: *The Future of Iraq* by Laurie Mylroie

#23: *"The Poor Man's Atomic Bomb?" Biological Weapons in the Middle East* by Seth Carus

#22: *Jerusalem* by Teddy Kollek

#21: *"The Sword of the Arabs": Iraq's Strategic Weapons* by Michael Eisenstadt

#20: *OPEC Ascendant? Another Case of Crying Wolf* by Eliyahu Kanovsky

#19: *In Through the Out Door: Jordan's Disengagement and the Peace Process* by Asher Susser

#18: *At Arm's Length: Soviet-Syrian Relations in the Gorbachev Era* by John Hannah

#17: *Unaffordable Ambitions: Syria's Military Build-Up and Economic Crisis* by Patrick Clawson

#16: *Hezbollah's Vision of the West* by Martin Kramer

#15: *Security for Peace: Israel's Minimal Security Requirements in Negotiations with the Palestinians* by Ze'ev Schiff

#14: *The Genie Unleashed: Iraq's Chemical and Biological Weapons Production* by Seth Carus

#13: *The PLO's New Policy: Evolution Until Victory* by Barry Rubin

#12: *Development Diplomacy: U.S. Economic Assistance to the West Bank and Gaza* by Joyce Starr

#11: *Changing the Balance of Risks: U.S. Policy Toward the Arab-Israeli Conflict* by Harvey Sicherman

#10: *Army and Politics in Mubarak's Egypt* by Robert Satloff

#9: *Formalizing the Strategic Partnership: The Next Step in U.S.-Israel Relations* by Stuart Eizenstat

#8: *Double Jeopardy: PLO Strategy Toward Israel and Jordan* by Asher Susser

#7: *Peace by Piece: A Decade of Egyptian Policy Toward Israel* by Ehud Ya'ari

#6: *Another Oil Shock in the 1990s? A Dissenting View* by Eliyahu Kanovsky

#5: *"They Cannot Stop Our Tongues": Islamic Activism in Jordan* by Robert Satloff

THE WASHINGTON INSTITUTE POLICY FOCUS SERIES

#33 *Islamism Across the Green Line: Relations Among Islamists in Israel, the West Bank, and Gaza* by Elie Rekhess

#32: *Jordan-Israel Peace: Taking Stock, 1994-1997* by Lori Plotkin

#31: *Israel and the Gulf: New Security Frameworks for the Middle East* by Dore Gold

#30: *Jordan-Israel Peace, Year One: Laying the Foundation* by Steven A. Cook

#29: *An Islamic Republic of Algeria? Implications for the Middle East and the West* by Gideon Gera

#28: *Extending the Nuclear Nonproliferation Treaty: The Middle East Debate* by Shai Feldman

#27: *Proliferation for Profit: North Korea in the Middle East* by Joseph S. Bermudez, Jr.

#26: *Tourism Cooperation in the Levant* by Patrick Clawson

#25: *Toward a Syrian-Israeli Peace Agreement: Perspective of a Former Negotiator* by Yossi Olmert

#24: *Peace Through Entrepreneurship: Practical Ideas from Middle Eastern Business Leaders* by Erturk Deger, M. Shafik Gabr, and Benjamin Gaon

#23: *Russian Arms Sales Policy Toward the Middle East* by Andrei Volpin

#22: *The Vindication of Sadat in the Arab World* by Saad Eddin Ibrahim

#21: *Iraq: Options for U.S. Policy* by Laurie Mylroie

#20: *Water and the Peace Process: Two Perspectives* by Shlomo Gur and Munther Haddadin

#19: *Hamas: The Fundamentalist Challenge to the PLO* by Clinton Bailey

#18: *Baghdad Between Shi'a and Kurds* by Ofra Bengio

#17: *The Arab States and the Arab-Israeli Peace Process: Linkage or Disengagement?* by Barry Rubin

#16: *Toward Middle East Peace Negotiations: Israeli Postwar Political-Military Options in an Era of Accelerated Change* by Dore Gold

#15: *Israel and the Gulf Crisis: Changing Security Requirements on the Eastern Front* by Dore Gold

#14: *Iraq's Economic and Military Vulnerabilities* by Patrick Clawson and Seth Carus

#13: *The Arab-Israeli Peace Process: A Trip Report* by Harvey Sicherman, Graeme Bannerman, Martin Indyk, and Samuel Lewis

#12: *Inside the PLO: Officials, Notables and Revolutionaries* by Barry Rubin

#11: *Palestinian Elections: Working Out the Modalitites* by Larry Garber

#10: *Toward Israeli-Palestinian Disengagement* by Ehud Ya'ari

#9: *Chemical Weapons in the Middle East* by W. Seth Carus

#8: *The PLO—A Declaration of Independence?* by Barry Rubin

#7: *Islam in the Palestinian Uprising* by Robert Satloff

#6: *Missiles in the Middle East: A New Threat to Stability* by W. Seth Carus

#5: *Behind the Riot in Mecca* by Martin Kramer

#4: *NATO, Israel, and the Tactical Missile Challenge* by W. Seth Carus

#3: *U.S.-Israel Strategic Cooperation*

#2: *Whither the Peace Process? The Local Leadership Option*

#1: *The Soviet Union and Mideast Diplomacy*

RECENT PUBLICATIONS OF THE WASHINGTON INSTITUTE

Building for Security and Peace in the Middle East: An American Agenda— A comprehensive blueprint for U.S. Middle East policy during the second Clinton administration from the Institute's bipartisan Presidential Study Group.

The Future of U.S.-Israel Strategic Cooperation—An examination by Shai Feldman of the origins of U.S.-Israel strategic cooperation and the ways in which the end of the Cold War and progress in the Arab-Israeli peace process can be used to build a closer, more integrated bilateral defense relationship in the years ahead.

Making Peace with the PLO: The Rabin Government's Road to the Oslo Accord—A detailed assessment of the personal, domestic, and international factors that led Yitzhak Rabin, Shimon Peres, and Israel's Labor government to conduct the secret negotiations that resulted in the historic Israeli-Palestinian peace accords, by *Ha'aretz* and *U.S. News and World Report* correspondent David Makovsky.

Supporting Peace: America's Role in an Israel-Syria Peace Agreement—A report by Michael Eisenstadt, Andrew Bacevich, and Carl Ford on the role that U.S. forces could play in monitoring and maintaining a future Israel-Syria peace agreement.

Approaching Peace: American Interests in Israeli-Palestinian Final Status Talks—A collection of essays presenting specific policy recommendations for Washington's role in reaching a final peace agreement. The contributors are Hermann Eilts, Richard Haass, Samuel Lewis, William Quandt, Peter Rodman, Eugene Rostow, Harvey Sicherman, and Kenneth Stein.

UN Security Council Resolution 242: The Building Block of Peacemaking—A collection of papers examining the resolution's history and relevance for current Arab-Israeli negotiations, by Adnan Abu Odeh, Nabil Elaraby, Meir Rosenne, Eugene Rostow, Dennis Ross, and Vernon Turner.

Democracy and Arab Political Culture—An examination by Elie Kedourie of the political traditions of Islam and the introduction of Western ideas into the Middle East in the 19th century.

The Politics of Change in the Middle East—A collection of essays by regional scholars examining political stability and regime succession, edited by Robert Satloff.

For a catalogue of Washington Institute publications, contact:

The Washington Institute *for Near East Policy*
1828 L Street, NW, Suite 1050
Washington, D.C. 20036
Phone (202) 452-0650 ◊ Fax (202) 223-5364
E-mail: info@washingtoninstitute.org
Internet: www.washingtoninstitute.org

THE WASHINGTON INSTITUTE
for Near East Policy
*An educational foundation supporting scholarly research
and informed debate on U.S. interests in the Near East*

President Michael Stein	**Executive Committee**	*Chairman* Barbi Weinberg
Charles Adler	*Vice Presidents* Robert Goldman	Walter P. Stern
Richard S. Abramson Richard Borow Benjamin Breslauer Maurice Deane	*Secretary/Treasurer* Fred Lafer	Leonard Goodman Roger Hertog Fred Schwartz Bernard S. White
Warren Christopher Alexander Haig Max M. Kampelman Jeane Kirkpatrick Edward Luttwak Michael Mandelbaum Robert C. McFarlane	**Board of Advisors** *Counselor* Samuel W. Lewis	Martin Peretz Richard Perle James Roche Eugene V. Rostow George P. Shultz Paul Wolfowitz Mortimer Zuckerman
Adjunct Scholars Patrick Clawson Hirsh Goodman Joshua Muravchik Daniel Pipes Harvey Sicherman	**Institute Staff** *Executive Director* Robert Satloff *Associates* Ze'ev Schiff	*Senior Fellows* Michael Eisenstadt Alan Makovsky *Research Fellow* Kenneth Pollack
Office Manager Nina Bisgyer	Ehud Ya'ari	*Associate Fellow* Hillary Mann
Director of Outreach Michael Grossman	*1997 Visiting Fellows* Abbas Kelidar Moshe Ma'oz Salay Meridor	*Scholar-in-Residence* Robert Danin
Development and Programs Anne van den Avond	Asher Susser Joshua Teitelbaum	*Director of Publications* John Wilner
Development Assistant Rebecca Medina	*National Defense Fellow* Lt. Col. Chuck Wilson, USAF	*Soref Fellows* Lori Plotkin Jonathan Torop
Financial Officer Laura Hannah	*Visiting Military Fellows* Lt. Col. Fuat Çalısır, Turkish Air Force Lt. Col. Dror Ben David, Israeli Air Force	*Research Assistants* Karen Dunn Hillary Ebenstein
Financial Assistant Patrick Garrett	*Research Interns* Megan Fisher	Eytan Fisch Stuart Frisch
Administrative Assistant Bill Tucker	Adam Frey Ami Wennar	Rachel Ingber Yonca Poyraz-Dogan